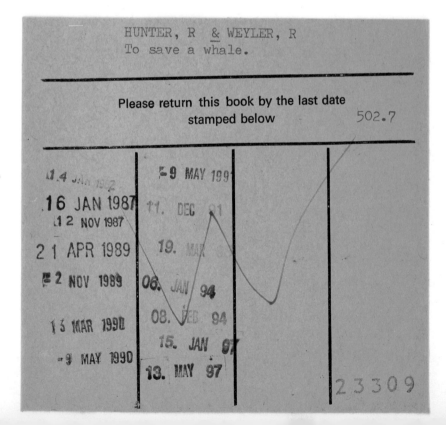

TO SAVE A WHALE
The Voyages of Greenpeace

Text: Robert Hunter
Photography: Rex Weyler
Introduction: Paul Spong

William Heinemann / London

Dedication: To Tusi, Bobbi, Glenn

Copyright © 1978
Text: Robert L. Hunter
Photographs: Rex Weyler

First UK edition published 1978
SBN 434-35620-4

23309
028561

**This book was produced under the
sign of the Scrimshaw Press**

William Heinemann Ltd.
15 Queen Street, Mayfair
London W1X 8BE

LONDON   MELBOURNE
JOHANNESBURG   AUKLAND

Introduction

THE WHALES, the *cetacea*: creatures of light, monsters of the deep, fuel for ancient lamps, aquatic acrobats, food for empty bellies, the biggest brains on the planet, twenty million years in the making, now on the anvil under the hammer of fate. Going, going, gone . . . nearly gone.

It is one of the ironies of our time that, just as we are beginning to marvel at the complexity of the nature of whales, we are on the verge of destroying them forever.

My own involvement with whales has a brief history—a decade or so. I was raised in New Zealand, a land once so blessed with whale populations that its first modern settlers were whalers. I spent the first years of my life in a little coastal community a few miles from Whale Island, a small mass of land shaped vaguely like a whale and the site of an early shore whaling station. I heard tales about famous New Zealand dolphins: Pelorus Jack, who guided vessels through treacherous waters for many years, and Opo, the friend of the bathers of Opononi. Yet I never saw a whale in the twenty-three years I lived in New Zealand. They had been virtually wiped out long before my time. It was not until 1970, in the coastal waters of British Columbia, that I first felt the joy of seeing a great whale alive in the ocean.

Trained as a physiological psychologist with a special curiosity about the relationship between brain systems and behavior, I readily snatched the opportunity to study whales when it was offered to me in 1967. The Vancouver Aquarium had recently acquired a young specimen of the species *Orcinus orca*, at that time commonly called the "Killer" whale but now familiar simply as "Orca." The aquarium needed a scientist to study the whale, named "Skana"—a Haida Indian word for whale—as the result of a name-finding contest. I was chosen. That decision was to shape my life.

Ten years ago virtually nothing was known about *Orcinus orca* beyond its reputation as a ferocious predator. And I myself knew almost nothing about whales, perhaps even less than is common knowledge these days. So I did some reading, talked with a renowned cetologist, Dr. Kenneth Norris (who happened to be on my campus), and formulated a research program which stressed investigation of the animal's vision.

Because I was aware that there was some controversy over the question of cetacean intelligence, I deliberately adopted a conservative scientific strategy and approached my subject from the outset as if she were an unknown mammalian life form, perhaps as complex as the laboratory rat. We would amass the basic data and, with luck, it might eventually be possible to approach the question of intelligence obliquely by exploring the complexity of information which the whale's brain could process.

We ran a series of visual discrimination learning experiments, using a standard two-choice situation. Pairs of stimulus cards with one and two lines were presented underwater. The whale had to learn to push one of two levers upward, with the one on the two-line side of the card yielding her half a herring from an automatic feeder. Skana proved to be a much slower learner than the average laboratory rat, taking hundreds of trials to solve the first of these problems. But once she understood, she proved a remarkably consistent and patient performer. Hundreds and thousands of trials were run without error. And we were learning too. It turned out that Skana, whose underwater vision seemed about as good as a cat's above water—and that is hardly as good as a human's—learned visual discrimination in a very stimulus-specific way. She responded to much smaller changes in visual stimuli, such as the width of the gap between two vertical black lines, than you or I would. We guessed that this characteristic of her vision would serve for quick identification of members of her own

Paul Spong greets Skana the "Killer Whale" at Vancouver Aquarium.

"pod" or family group in the ocean through details such as the shape of their white head patches or dorsal fins.

At this point my own position in the procedure was, quite deliberately, distant. The tradition is that a scientist should remain remote from the subject of inquiry. So I remained in my laboratory and we controlled the experiment by logic circuitry. Assistants often ran the experiment and I had merely to contemplate the learning curves and wait. Ho-hum.

Then, one day, a remarkable thing happened, unprecedented in the annals of behavioral science. In one trial (that is, from one response to the next) Skana's performance switched from 100 percent to 0 percent correct, and remained there. She refused to punch the proper lever. She had quite clearly and consciously said "no!" We decided to call the phenomenon a "spontaneous reversal." It had two effects: first, it ruined our statistics and made it impossible for us to obtain the visual acuity data we had been seeking. More important, it forced me to step aside from the immediate experiment and look at the entire situation. Perhaps there was insufficient motivation for the whale to perform correctly. Half a long-dead herring might not mean much to a five-thousand pound whale. I thought about other motivational matters—perhaps the whale was bored because of the monotony of performing seventy-two nearly identical actions on cue at the same time each day for months on end.

It might be that she would be willing to perform "correctly" if she got the chance to do something different, such as swimming around the pool in a certain way or retrieving a ball. We tried some changes and they half-worked. Skana's performance returned to about 50 percent correct—better, but still not good enough for our beloved statistics. The experiment was abandoned. I dropped my posture of remoteness, opened my mind, and personally engaged myself in Skana's learning.

A joyous period of mutual exploration quickly began between the human and the animal. It seemed that Skana was as interested in learning about me as I was in her. Rapidly we began to gather a clearer idea of the creature's mind. This whale was no big-brained rat or mouse. She was more like a person: inquisitive, inventive, joyous, gentle, joking, patient, and, above all, unafraid and exquisitely self-controlled.

I learned huge amounts during this time of open-ended exploration. As one might have expected of an acoustically-sensitive creature, sound, especially music, was of great interest to her and useful to us. By this time I was also working with a juvenile male Orca named Hyak and saw that they both could be trained to perform a task for an aural reward. By observing the whales' responses to the sources of various sound stimuli I learned something of the organization of their acoustic systems. It seemed that the Orca had several paths of sound-reception, the most sensitive being the tips of the upper and lower jaws. I discovered that Orcas experience emotions and that the more intense of these are reflected in increased surface temperatures in the region of the head, to the point of the animal's giving off steam under certain conditions. Most important, I learned to trust them.

We saw too that there were severe limitations to the study of whales held as captives in concrete pools. They are acoustic social creatures, born to a world of unlimited sounds of the sea and their own kind. Their removal into solitude and silence in a confined space, with their own mocking echoes, must produce wholesale behavior changes in them. To understand the whole creature, we obviously had to go out into the ocean where the whale lives, breathes, loves, and dies, and study it there.

In the summer of 1970, my family and I, with the help of friends, established a field observation station on a small island in the coastal waters of British Columbia at a place

Greenpeace musicians serenade Skana.

where we were told Orcas would pass close to shore. We began a series of summer studies which continues today.

As we had earlier with the captives, we began our new work with full scientific detachment. Now, though, we were prepared for surprises. We placed hydrophones in the water so that we could hear and record the sounds of whales, and settled down in a lab among the trees overlooking the water. We routinely noted the passage of pods by our post, recorded the sounds they exchanged, timed their respiratory rhythms, and tried to count the numbers in each pod. There seemed to be about fifty and we were slowly learning more about them. But I found myself devoting more of my time to equipment than observation, and made the decision to step aside from technology again, in favor of closer contact with the whales.

One day in the summer of 1971 remains in my memory vivid as the finest stained glass. In a one-person kyak of Inuit design I paddled among a pod of whales and with astonishment and joy found myself immediately accepted. In the days and weeks that followed I spent many hours at a time with these new friends, coming to know some of them as individuals and beginning to learn something of their existence in the freedom of the seas. I was deeply moved by the effortless flow of their lives and by the close-knit cooperative organization of their social order. In succeeding years many of us have passed time in small craft with the whales, observing and communicating whenever possible. As I write this, I am ready to return to a technological approach, based on our learning and our presumption that the whales are willing to learn at the same time we are.

In 1972 I met the Canadian author Farley Mowat, whose books on wildlife have entertained, enthralled, and involved a whole generation. He was on a tour to promote his latest work, *A Whale for the Killing*, and his latest cause, the plight of the whales. A few months earlier the first United Nations Conference on the Human Environment had met in Stockholm and had unanimously called for an immediate end to commercial whaling. At that time I was largely ignorant of the desperate situation faced by most species of great whales and the growing struggle to save them. My interest had been solely a quest for knowledge. The meeting with Mowat changed this perception. I was seized with the obligation of those who *know*—the obligation to act. My wife-companion, Linda, and I deliberately put ourselves into the save-the-whales battle. We circulated petitions and tried to arouse the press and radio and television media, hoping to move the Canadian government to action. Just before Christmas of 1972 we received a marvelous present, largely I suppose because of Farley Mowat's personal contact with Canadian Prime Minister Trudeau, but also because of an aroused public. The Canadian government announced an end to whaling in Canada and immediate support for a ten-year moratorium on all commercial whaling.

In 1972 I also met Bob Hunter, ecology columnist for the *Vancouver Sun*. Bob learned of the plight of the whales and wanted to help. By 1973 we were contemplating the usefulness of guerilla action. Bob's idea was that unless we were already too late, direct intervention in whaling operations, on behalf of the whales, would have to swing the balance in their favor.

By the time of this writing two Greenpeace missions have confronted the whaling fleets on the high seas. These dramatic and nonviolent actions, in which human bodies have shielded whales from harpoons, have saved the lives of many whales and have focused worldwide attention on the Greenpeace campaigns. The story of those voyages is the subject of this book. A third mission is now being prepared and will have ended before these words are read and these photographs examined. I fervently hope that it will have succeeded, bringing an end to the needless slaughter of our gentle ocean friends. Time is running out. Tomorrow will be too late for the whales.

Paul Spong
1976

The *Phyllis Cormack* at rest in Winter Harbour

Our Beginnings

INTO AKUTAN BAY we chugged. The hills rose around us so that we seemed to be in the mouth of a wide, deep, crater. On the lower slopes of the hills, the grass grew no more than knee-high. We saw no trees, but only moss and fungus clinging to the rocks with clumps of heather between. Streams came drooling from far up the hill, close to the clouds, as though the whole island were a giant frozen sponge, squeezed by an invisible fist. Great clouds were spilling down toward us like slow-motion silent avalanches. The scale was so enormous, so disorienting, that we could imagine ourselves arriving on another planet.

As we steamed toward our anchorage, the clouds slowly swelled and swept downward, hanging like a cowl, and at a certain point in their descent they seemed to pause, mysteriously held back. Later I tried to put a label on the scene, calling them the surf-clouds of Akutan. They were like mile-high glaciers such as you might see from ground level in a film that had been sped up so that geological ages were compressed into seconds.

We anchored at the end of the bay, about a quarter of a mile from shore, where there was a rotted and broken dock, a pile of rust-covered machinery, the remains of several buildings, and five large water tanks or fuel tanks, whichever they were. The surf-clouds hung about a mile up the slope beyond. With the ship at rest, the silence that came to us quieted whatever anybody had to say. It was as though we had all suddenly received a command to remove our hats and get down for a moment on our knees.

It was early October in 1971. We were en route, we thought, to the remote Aleutian Island of Amchitka, where the U.S. Atomic Energy Commission was planning to trigger an underground nuclear blast. Our plan was to park our chartered vessel—an ancient eighty-foot halibut seiner—within three miles of Ground Zero, thus making the test all but impossible without the risk of us being blown out of the water or sprayed with vented radiation.

It was a good plan. Ours was a Canadian vessel. The Americans could not seize it in international waters without committing an act of piracy. But we were already in trouble. The test had been delayed a month, forcing us to put into Akutan, the easternmost major island in the chain extending almost to Russia. Within a week, although we had not yet guessed it, we would be arrested by the U.S. Coast Guard and sent packing back to Canada. We would never get to Amchitka.

Instead, we were to encounter something that was to move us even more deeply than our dread of nuclear Armageddon. Unknowingly, we had anchored next to an abandoned whaling station, one of the hundreds which dot the shores of the Aleutians, Alaska, and British Columbia.

Crossing the Gulf of Alaska westward on a great circle route from far down Prince Rupert to Akutan Pass, we had not seen a single whale. Our captain, John Cormack, a veteran fisherman who had traveled these waters for over forty years, had remarked, "Used to be, when you came out here on the Gulf, you could see them whales from horizon to horizon. They'd come up to the boat like big puppies. 'Course you don't see them any longer. They're *extinct*."

It had been gray and lonely and oppressive out on the Gulf. The captain's words rang in our ears. They gave a new dimension of despair to our action. We had been filled for years with the fear that the human race might wipe itself out through nuclear weaponry. Our efforts to try to save ourselves and to spare our children had seemed such an urgent matter. Now it seemed that saving human lives was somehow not quite enough. There was a sense that some major point had been missed, that incalculable damage had already been done, and that we were, in some fundamental way, too late.

The whaling station might have been in operation as little as thirty years earlier, perhaps right up to the onset of the Second World War. But aeons had passed and none of us was quite prepared for the mood of devastation that clung to the dock and the tumbled buildings. The wooden sheds lay scattered in heaps like smashed furniture. Incomprehensible machinery mellowed in rust, growing out of pockets of loam which had collected where it could. Lichen dwelled in beautiful patterns on the walls of engines. The wind played among pulleys and pipes which had not yet been covered by soil or seashell debris.

The wind tugged at our scarves and jackets. No one tried to speak. We separated, each to wander alone. Somehow the ruins seemed to have more to do with our own future than with the long-dead whales. Perhaps we were thinking of the thermonuclear bomb being fashioned only a few hundred miles away.

There was a spot near the water tanks where the ground was level, almost a swamp. At first it looked like one of those little bays, heaped with driftwood, with soil and sand and pebbles and shell jewelry from the sea, and a few chunks of wooden debris sticking up through the surface. Except that there are no trees, and therefore no driftwood, in the Aleutian Islands.

Bones. They were like dry pulp, their surfaces pitted with tiny holes. Ribs stuck up like parts of an old picket fence. Vertebrae the size of toilet bowls lay half-buried, barely visible through clumps of horsetail rush. Part of a jawbone jabbed out of the ground like a gray sheet of plywood.

There was nothing to indicate that these immense ribcages and spines and skulls had been torn from a whale at all. Perhaps they came from people. Had I not known the place to have been a whaling station, I would automatically have fantasized that these were the remains of a giant Man. I would have thought that we had stumbled across the smashed skeletons of a race that had stood sixty or seventy feet tall, on an ancient battlefield where titans had been torn apart. What awful creatures could have materialized out of the fogs and surf-clouds to dismember the giants as though they were less than toys? It was enough to fill a primitive man with terror and to send him fleeing back to his boat, before the super-monster could appear to gobble up another morsel.

Otherwise there was only the island, looking as it must have looked a million years ago, two million years ago, with its eroded hills, its sweeps of grass, the gray line of the bay. The colors all blended, the shapes running together in some inexpressible harmony, and I could hear the gulls, flying above the beach, *ky-ky-ky-ky.*

Out in the bay, our battered old seiner looked like nothing much more than a toy itself. It had taken so much effort just to get this far, and while we had not yet reached the gateway to the bomb, it seemed we had come to some other, unexpected, gateway. The silence spoke as clearly as the roar we had been bracing ourselves to hear. The holocaust that was coming seemed, for the moment, to hold no more horror than the holocaust that had already come.

Fog drapes the northwest coast of
Vancouver Island near Winter
Harbour.

New Directions

The sail on our boat was dark green. On it, painted in a yellow that had already been blackened by soot from the stack, was the word we had chosen to express our goal: *Greenpeace*.

We began as the Don't Make A Wave Committee, a coalition of West Coast environmentalists and antiwar protesters. The name *Greenpeace* was chosen temporarily for the vessel that would sail to Amchitka simply because the word nicely expressed the spirit of both the ecology and the peace movements. It was not until the boat was almost back home in Vancouver that the decision was made to rename the organization and start preparing for another attempt in the following year to sail into the Amchitka bomb test zone. Thus, a new name: The Greenpeace Foundation.

Before the new group could even begin to form its plan for a second assault on Amchitka, the U.S. government announced that no further tests would be carried out there. The island was to be turned into a game sanctuary. The Greenpeace voyage, as well as other forms of protest, had generated enough political pressure that the Pentagon decided that Amchitka was too vulnerable a test site and closed down the operation.

The Greenpeace Foundation immediately turned its attention to French nuclear tests in the South Pacific. In the spring of 1972 a group sailed a small ketch into the test zone at Mururoa Atoll, where it was rammed by a French navy minesweeper and towed away. The vessel returned to the site in 1973. Its owner was beaten with rubber truncheons, suffering permanent damage to his right eye. But the action succeeded in triggering a storm of international protests. By the spring of 1975, the French government had halted its atmospheric tests at Mururoa, just as the Americans had closed their underground facilities at Amchitka three years earlier. In both cases, Greenpeace ships had provided a spearhead of opposition.

As soon as the news came through that France had abandoned its atmospheric nuclear program, Greenpeace began to develop the idea that had been slumbering in the backs of our minds ever since that October day in the Aleutian Islands amid the ruins of the whaling station. We had often sent boats into atomic test areas for the sake of human life. Now, with Amchitka left in peace and the nuclear monster driven down into the darkness beneath the coral at Mururoa, we might send a boat out to defend the sacredness of another awesome kind of life.

With the announcement in January, 1975, that the Greenpeace Foundation would attempt to go to the rescue of the world's last remaining great whales, a frightening energy became available to us. Earlier, pitting ourselves against the bomb, we had acted in the defense of our own homes, our own land, our own people. There was nothing really new about it. The bomb itself might provoke terror, and even a sense of awe, but it was finally nothing more than another human invention. There had been great energy spent to protest the atomic testing, but that was merely war; now our campaign for the whales became religion.

Compared to a great whale, even a nuclear bomb is just a gadget. In announcing that we would put ourselves between the harpoon and the whale—that we were willing to die to save the whales—we committed ourselves to something greater than anything we had undertaken before. We had committed ourselves finally to something that was greater than the human

In January 1975 we held our first meetings
to plan an antiwhaling campaign.

race itself. It was as though a moment had come for us to crawl up out of some dark sea and perceive a whole new world on the horizon. Suddenly it seemed so simple. If there was to be any salvation on this planet, it was not enough to shield human beings from their own folly. We would have to shield the non-humans too, for without them there would be a weakening and deterioration of the great system of order underlying the whole flow of life on the planet.

At first, the idea of sending a Greenpeace boat out to try to intercept the whaling fleets was greeted by scepticism and scorn. It caused a major rift among Greenpeace veterans themselves, many of whom thought the whaling issue to be frivolous in comparison to the problem of nuclear weapons. Some others in the group rejected the idea on the grounds that finding the whaling fleets in the vastness of the ocean would be utterly impossible for it was no longer a matter of setting a course for an island or atoll, however remote. This time we would be seeking a moving target. One Greenpeace advisor, a former U.S. Navy captain, said flatly: "It's too big an ocean and those guys can move at twenty knots. You haven't got a chance."

Indeed, at the early stages of organization, it was difficult to avoid the feeling that we had passed into some crazy New Age fantasy world. On previous expeditions there had been a hard core of veteran seamen, former military men, and toughened antiwar protesters. Most of them withdrew, not wanting to be associated with what they thought of as a "hippie thing."

At the time we announced our plan, we did not, in fact, have a clue as to where the fleets might be found. We thought vaguely that they might be operating near the Sea of Okhotsk northeast of Japan. Or perhaps they were somewhere off the west coast of Canada. It was not a strong basis on which to launch any kind of an expedition and if were going to carry on in the face of such odds, it could only be as an act of faith. From a purely rational point of view, the whole exercise was hopeless.

During this initial stage of doubt and misgiving, it was due to the conviction of one man that we were able to carry on. That man was Dr. Paul Spong, an expatriate New Zealand physiological psychologist, who had spent a year studying a captive whale named Skana at the Vancouver Public Aquarium. Paul's studies, like those of John Lilly, led him to the conclusion that the whales possessed a high order of awareness, comparable to, if not superior to, humanity's. It was Paul Spong, more than any other person, who put us on the track of saving the whales and kept us on the track. It was Paul who convinced the doubters among us, who shored up the faith that repeatedly crumbled. He never wavered: "You can count on help from the whales."

This belief was to be our secret ace in the hole, our only ace, for we knew that the chances of finding the whaling fleets were just about zero. We knew that, even if we found them, they would be able to move so much more swiftly than we could that the chances of successful interference amounted to yet another zero. We knew that on all counts the undertaking was irrational and futile, unless . . . unless Paul Spong was right.

And so, from the beginning, we were embarked on a quest no less mystical than the search for the Holy Grail. It would take the equivalent of a twelfth-century miracle for it to work. Yet, when we accepted the fact that we were looking for a

A facelift (above) for the *Phyllis Cormack* and, on the right, Barry Lavendar selling hard for Greenpeace

Henry Payne, the mystic who donated
five acres of land for a Greenpeace
raffle

miracle, and nothing less, it brought people to us in droves. And not just in random droves—if we needed an electronics expert, one would appear. If we needed a shipwright, a shipwright would show up at the next meeting. If we decided we needed a musician, or a photographer or an engineer, they, too, would appear as though on cue. It was either a grand illusion or else some kind of psychic tom-tom was at work in the jungle of the collective unconscious. It was impossible to avoid the feeling that we were in harmony with a force so much greater than ourselves that no one dared to talk about it. We simply lived it.

There is a centuries-old Cree Indian prophecy that says a time will come at last when the birds are dropping from the sky, the rivers poisoned, and the deer dying in the forests, when the white man's greed and technology have all but destroyed Mother Earth. At that time, the Indian people will find their lost spirit and communicate it to the other races. Together, as warriors of the Rainbow, these people will go forth to restore the sense of the sacred. A great part of our inspiration, from the beginning, came from this Indian prophecy.

It was therefore not surprising to find, in short order, that we had been joined by numerous nature mystics, shamans, Indian revolutionaries, Buddhist monks and even a renegade Brahman from India. From the Kwakiutl Indians of British Columbia's west coast we borrowed an image of the whale which became our symbol and our banner. By "coincidence" the head of the oldest school of Tibetan Buddhism, Gyalwa Karmapa XIV, a man believed by his followers to be the personification of the Divine Compassion, showed up in Vancouver and, told of our plans, announced that such effort "is in accord with the will of the Buddha." He gave us his personal blessing. A white-haired mystic, who lived in an old wooden shack in east Vancouver, emerged from his retreat to donate five acres of land which we were allowed to raffle off to raise money. He promised as well to control the weather for us so that we could not be stopped.

All this was a bit too bizarre for the existing conservation organizations, so we soon found ourselves operating on the outer edge of the environmental movement. It did not seem to matter that we had at least four Ph.D.'s working closely with us. Nor did it seem to make much difference that our crew was going to include people from Japan, France, England, Australia, New Zealand, Czechoslovakia, the United States and Canada. Or that we had electronics experts, navigators, oceanographers, divers, doctors, and lawyers involved as well. We were definitely on the fringes of respectability.

It was a fine, if unconventional, blend of human talents and skills. There were, as well, dozens of people who regularly consulted the *I Ching*, astrology charts, and ancient Aztec tables. Yet for every mystic there was at least one mechanic, and salty old west coast experts on diesel engines and boat hulls showed up at the early meetings to sit next to young vegetarian women. Hippies and psychologists mixed freely with animal lovers, poets, musicians, marine surveyors, housewives, ballet dancers, computer programmers, biologists, and photographers.

We set up a trust fund, organized several benefit concerts, a raffle, and started selling buttons, T-shirts, posters and bumper stickers, using volunteers ranging in age from six to seventy years. By April of 1975 we had worked out an arrangement with John C. Cormack, the tough old captain who had taken us up to the Aleutian Islands in 1971, to make use of his eighty-foot halibut seiner, *Phyllis Cormack*, again. A second skipper, a silver-haired former law professor and Second World War pilot named Jacques Longini, had volunteered the use of his own sailing vessel, *Vega*, which meant that we could theoretically cover twice the area of ocean which we could otherwise patrol.

The fact remained, however, that our lead vessel could make only a maximum of ten knots, and the sailing vessel only seven with a good stiff wind behind it. Our total range was obviously less than a tiny portion of the North Pacific. And so while we had succeeded in raising money and attracting the attention of the media, the essential ingredient was very much still lacking. How were we ever to find the fleets?

Most of the people closely involved in the process of creating a reality out of our fantasy—to actually find a way to get our bodies out onto the ocean and save some whales—were firmly of two minds as to what was happening. With one mind it was easy to see that we were involved in the flowering of an inevitable miracle. The weather itself seemed to be on our side. The things that were needed, appeared. When a certain kind of talent became essential, some individual or another materialized on our doorstep. We seemed definitely blessed. Certainly we *felt* blessed.

But with the other mind, we could see clearly that what faced us was simply an enormous amount of work: hours and hours and hours of hassles to find parts for an engine, paint for a deck, guarantors to sign for a loan, all of that and more. (Yes, we raised most of the money by borrowing from a bank. Protest now, pay later.) At that level, the first five months of 1975 were a burn-out. No fewer than three hundred people showed up at one time or another to volunteer their services. We went through them, exhausting their energies, in weeks. Only a hard core of about one dozen people held the project together, and the toll, psychologically, was dreadful. Seven of our brothers became so mentally and emotionally drained that they ended under sedation in hospitals or else behind bars. It was a disorganized attack, deeply inspired and trembling with high levels of energy, but incredibly wasteful.

By April 27, we came to the end of what seemed to have been a very long and frantic journey—the point where the first antiwhaling expedition was about to be launched. There had been a tremendous storm the night before. It left broken telephone poles and ships smashed against their docks. Rooftops had been shredded. Yet on the morning of the day Greenpeace was to set sail the light came clear for the first time in months. Rainbows appeared over the bay. With twenty thousand people cheering us as we set out from the beach to our ships in a recycled Army landing craft, there was nothing that we could feel except that we were on our way to an ecological crusade.

By this time, we had acquired the one single piece of critical information we needed—the routes of the Russian and Japanese whaling fleets. Paul Spong traveled all the way to Europe to infiltrate the headquarters of the International Whaling Commission. There, using a subterfuge, he obtained copies of charts showing where both fleets had gone during the previous two years. It was the first real evidence we had that our long shot might work, for there was at least one place along the old route of the Russian fleet where we might actually reach them. And in June, less than sixty miles off the coast of California. It was the only point where either fleet was likely to come within our limited range.

The *Phyllis Cormack* ready to go

The Summer of '75

Fearing that the Russian whaling fleet might decide to slip in close to the California coast earlier than usual, in order to avoid us, we allowed ourselves a two-month head start. This would also give us time to carry out an experiment which we had earlier regarded as a secondary purpose of the voyage but was now becoming more and more important to us: we would try to communicate with the whales, as equals, in their own environment.

Under the guidance of Dr. John Lilly, we constructed a sound system designed to meet all the requirements of an exercise in interspecies communication. This involved the construction of underwater loudspeakers and the installation of a generator to broadcast some two hundred hours of classical music at ten times its normal speed. We had also acquired hydrophones to record the response of the whales, but the key ingredient was to be the presence of live human musicians. Experiments carried out by Paul Spong and others along the West Coast showed that whales respond positively to music *and* to the personality of the musician, so we arranged to have several musicians on board. Our group included a San Francisco Moog synthesizer player named Will Jackson, whose electronic soundmaker could be hooked up to the underwater broadcasting system to attempt to duplicate whale sounds, and flutist Paul Horn, saxophone player Paul Winter, singer Don Francks, and our onboard musician, Melville Gregory, selected because his specialty was animal affinity.

Our first attempts to communicate with the whales came off the west coast of Vancouver Island where we tracked down a pod of seven gray whales. While the whales did not particularly respond to us, they did allow our crew to get so close that at one point a big gray lifted one of our rubber rafts right out of the water on its flukes and then gently dropped it back into the sea without an injury. Later we encountered *Orcinus orca*, and this time the "killers" allowed us to move into the middle of their pod to serenade them.

The net effect of these encounters was to leave us so free of fear of the whales that several crew members dove into the water to swim with leviathan and each one came back reporting that the closer he got to the whales, the higher he felt. Not a single whale made any kind of menacing movement.

There was a kind of positive tension surrounding the expedition that was quite different from any protest I had ever joined or observed. For one thing, nobody on either of the two Greenpeace vessels thought of himself (or herself) as a protester as such. There was a feeling, instead, that we were engaged in a righteous, positive, battle. There was also something odd about the voyage which was hard to pin down, but it had to do with the presence of photographers and a film crew on board. During moments of crisis—problems with the sails, sudden changes in weather, unexpected situations that required swift decision-making—a part of the crew withdrew from the action, thrusting cameras and microphones toward the rest of us.

The entire Greenpeace whale voyage was being filmed to make a feature-length documentary to be distributed around the world. The movie would be an extension of the voyage itself. Its aim was to pass on to as many people as possible the message we were trying to communicate: stop killing the whales. It also meant that whatever other problems they were facing, the crew had to cope with the idea that each person's actions were being documented. There was little that we would be able to hide. If we failed ourselves or changed our thinking at any point along the way, that too would become a matter of public record.

At moments, the voyage seemed dreamlike, as though it were already a movie and we were all actors playing our various parts, yet at the same time everything was overpoweringly real. The sea was no illusion. The boats themselves were solid and they moved with undeniable violence when the winds came up. And there was, inside everyone's gut, a certain tightness that came from thinking ahead to the ultimate moment when we would come face-to-face with the Russian whalers.

There were problems, a seemingly endless string of problems. But they were solved one by one. Most important, nobody was daunted by the difficulties. Each new problem that was overcome led us to a strengthening of the belief that, whatever happened next, we would be able to handle it. In a word, we carried a great charge of confidence, despite the odds against successful achievement of our goal.

Few expeditions of any kind could have had crews as oddly assorted as ours. There was Nicholas Desplats, a pipe-smoking young French ecologist whose group, Friends of the Earth, had helped in the campaign against French nuclear testing in the South Pacific. The crew included George Korotva, a Czechoslovakian psychologist who spoke fluent Russian. Since coming to Canada, Korotva had signed on as skipper of a 120-foot vessel operating out of Tofino, B.C., and he contributed heavily to steadying the crew's nerves during the chaotic first days of the voyage. Several Americans contributed a variety of skills and expertise, including Ramon Falkowski of San Jose, who sailed on the yacht *Fri* which pushed into the French nuclear testing zone at Mururoa Atoll in 1973, and Matt Herron of Palo Alto who served as navigator. A photojournalist who was deeply involved in the civil rights and antiwar movements in the United States, Herron's qualifications included having sailed a small boat from Florida to Africa, a voyage which was documented in a book he and his family wrote, *The Voyage of Aquarius.* Herron also doubled as sailing master.

Another American was Gary Zimmerman, a member of the Oceanic Society, responsible for constructing what was probably a very sophisticated shark cage which could be lowered or raised in the water by inflatable devices. As an experienced scuba diver, Zimmerman was to swim among the whales and attempt to get underwater film footage of the aftermath of a harpoon killing when there might be sharks present in large numbers. The rest of the crew was composed of Canadians, mainly from British Columbia and it included two women, Carlie Trueman of Victoria, an experienced scuba diver and small-craft operator, and Taeko Miwa, our Japanese translator.

We were also grateful to have Dr. Patrick Moore of Winter Harbour, an ecologist who was trained at the University of British Columbia, and Walrus Oakenbough, a nutritionist who served as cook and who was one of the few white persons to be allowed by the Oglala Sioux to join in the Indian seizure of Wounded Knee, South Dakota, in 1973. The crew also included cameraman and soundman Fred Easton and Ron Precious of Vancouver.

At an early stage of planning for the expedition, a few people were asked not to come to meetings because they had displayed what many Greenpeacers thought to be racist behavior. Instead, many Vancouverites of Japanese origin and Japanese nationals themselves were invited to take part. This paid off in important respects, because it would now be possible for Greenpeace to deal with any Japanese whalers in terms that they could understand.

Both Greenpeace vessels flew the United Nations flag at their mastheads, above the Canadian flag and above the Greenpeace flags. A number of people on board the boats carried what are known as "planetary passports," not yet recognized by many governments but representative of a growing movement to establish a clear sense of world identity instead of the age-old national or tribal identity which serves to divide people against one another.

The ship's cook, Walrus Oakenbough
(left) and the captain (above) at
breakfast

Greenpeace is at sea at last.

Above, Don Franks plays for an Orca near Bella Bella. Below, it's Paul Winter for some grays off Vancouver Island.

A Paul Winter–Mel Gregory duet and
gray whales, the ideal audience

Will Jackson and Captain Cormack load
extra fuel tanks into the hold. On the
right, Taeko Miwa, our Japanese
interpreter

On watch for whales and whalers

Mel Gregory at the wheel under the
captain's eye and (right) Bob Hunter
in his engine room office

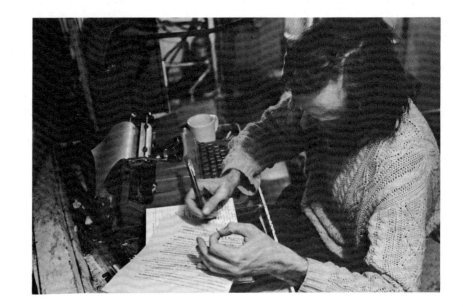

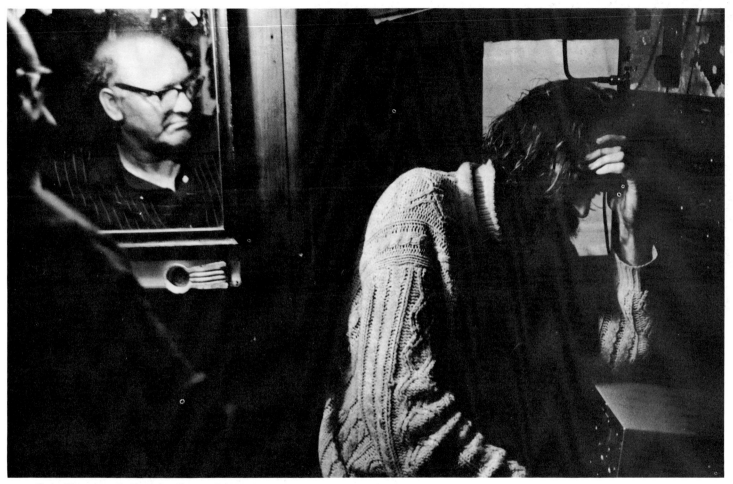

Bob Hunter and Captain Cormack
struggle to communicate with
Vancouver on the ship's radio.

Will Jackson plays the synthesizer under
a gibbous moon. Right: Korotva, Moore,
Hewitt, and Oakenbough work the charts.

Chasing the Russian fleet southwestward

We Meet the Russians

After leaving Vancouver's Jericho Beach on April 27 the crews of both Greenpeace vessels found themselves being put through what were, for us, some very real psychological and physical ordeals. An attack of appendicitis hit crewman Paul Watson, the man chosen to handle the inflatable raft which would be driven directly between the Russian harpoons and the fleeing whales. He had been preparing himself for months and it seemed like a piece of rotten luck for him to be knocked out so early in the voyage. He swiftly recovered, however, and rejoined the crew at the beginning of June in time for the expected confrontation. His appendicitis came at a time when three other crewmen, Brian Small, George Korotva, and myself, were being hit by dental problems and, in Small's case, a fever which resulted in his being taken off the ship to a shore hospital.

At that early stage of the voyage, all of our emotions were on edge. The Jericho launching had been as moving as it was successful. Not only was the crowd of supporters and well-wishers gigantic but almost everybody in the crew found himself running into dozens of old friends, relatives, and loved ones. It turned out to be more a fantastic reunion than a farewell, bringing everyone close together and at the same time recalling many old feelings and a powerful sense of obligation to everyone present. At least two crew members found themselves, at the last minute, too choked up with feelings to be able to talk. Several others found themselves in the embrace of their families, quite unabashedly crying.

For days after we sailed, few of the crewmembers could get down to work. We had been too moved by the last-minute rush of feeling. "I have never felt so much love coming at me as I did that day we took off," commented musician Melville Gregory. "Love is wonderful, but it's like everything else. If a giant wave of it hits you, it knocks you over, that's all."

In the afterglow of the Jericho launch, most people on board the Greenpeace ships found that they had to take a deep breath and steady themselves. The realization dawned on every crew member that he or she was now carrying the burden of many people's hopes, and perhaps the fate of the whales themselves. It took several days for them to "come down" enough to start performing their specialized functions properly.

But by then a practical approach to the voyages was inevitable. Step by step we had to learn whether sophisticated electronic equipment would actually operate reliably under the hostile conditions of the sea. We had to face the inevitable nervousness which comes over any landlubber out on the ocean as well as the awful matter of seasickness—would we live or wouldn't we? And it is a fact that the waters off the west coast of Vancouver Island are the graveyard of hundreds of vessels. The toll taken by spring storms in 1975, especially among herring boats, had been high.

The seaworthiness of both Greenpeace vessels quickly came to be tested. Some 200 miles out in the ocean *Vega* found herself having to reef the sails and ride out what local fishermen later described as one of the worst storms since winter. Winds up to 45 m.p.h. sent the ketch flying, almost spinning, through waves that heaved over the decks, leaving the impression at times that the boat was really a submarine. Meanwhile the larger seiner, *Phyllis Cormack*, was being battered by the same storm 250 miles to the south. At one point virtually the entire crew was seasick.

Both vessels proved to be as sturdy and reliable as the organizers of the campaign had hoped. Delicate electronics equipment proved to be readily thrown out of kilter, but the presence on board the *Cormack* of Alan Hewitt, a Vancouver electronics expert, described by numerous people as nothing less than a genius, made the difference between disaster and success. He sometimes had to come up with wholly improvised and unheard of ways of repairing equipment and at one point, for instance, had to take an oscilloscope apart—salt water had leaked into its circuitry—and wash parts of it in fresh water, later drying them out over the galley stove before reassembling the apparatus.

After two months at sea, we were a shaggy and dry-mouthed crew. Our bread and margarine supply had been ruined by a diesel oil spill in the hold which soaked into one of the food compartments. We had already run out of canned juice, coffee, tailormade cigarettes and vegetables. Water had been on ration for a week. The bunkroom stank, and nobody had been able to wash except in salt water.

Our radio communication with Vancouver had all but completely broken down, so that while we could just make out voices coming to us from home through wild chatterings of static, our friends ashore could hear nothing at all from us except bursts of inhuman noise. As the communications officer on board, my throat was raw from yelling through the microphone of Captain Cormack's twenty-five-year-old Northern radiophone. And once we had pushed farther than 600 miles from Vancouver, our newly-installed single sideband radio failed us entirely. Several of us were physically exhausted from the violent pitching and rolling of the *Phyllis Cormack*.

On Monday, June 23, the day that the International Whaling Commission meeting opened in London, our Russian translator, George Korotva, overheard a complete radio transmission taking place between the 450-foot Soviet factory ship, *Dalniy Vostok*, and one of its fleet of harpoon boats, the 150-foot *Charadinski*. The *Dalniy Vostok* at that point was still far to the west of us and the signal from the *Charadinski* was too feeble for our radio direction finder to get a fix. Then on Thursday evening, June 26—the third day of the whaling commission meeting—translator Korotva suddenly jumped from the corner of the galley where he had been slumped wearily listening to radio signals. His face was transformed. "That's them! That's them!"

Electronics technician Hewitt got an RDF fix on the signal. Dr. Moore took a Loran reading to establish our position and the position of the Russian ship which was about sixty miles off the northern California coast. We altered course immediately, bearing closer toward land.

That night we bucked heavy seas, traveling at full speed. Tossed about in our bunks, having to listen to bursts of static and Russian voices over the radio, none of us got anything more than snatches of sleep. In the morning, almost everyone reported having had weird and disturbing dreams. By 10:00 A.M., there could be no doubt; we could see the huge factory ship, *Dalniy Vostok*, on the horizon, and between us and the *Dalniy Vostok*, moving in circles like a pack of predators on the trail of their prey, were the harpoon boats. Hard-edged, military, the harpoons were indistinguishable in the distance from cannons. It was like coming upon a scene in a war movie. It was the last day of the International Whaling Commission meeting.

Within only a few miles of the nearest harpoon boat we came across a small dead sperm whale, its intestines trailing out, blood diffused in the water like a pink cloud all around. A radio antenna and a radar reflector were attached to the spear in its side.

"My God, it's just a baby!" cried Carlie Trueman.

A Russian killer boat has left a radio
beacon and a radar reflector attached
to a sperm whale carcass.

Our emotions were running high, sweeping us along on gouts of adrenalin. Less than two miles away, a Russian harpooner was spinning around with the dexterity of a PT boat, preparing to charge toward us. Within minutes, we had four people circling the dead whale in a rubber boat. Crewman Watson clambered over it, getting data to compare later with photographs for an accurate length measurement. They were shielded by the bulk of the *Phyllis Cormack*, but the Russian vessel was bearing down on us rapidly. A figure appeared at the bow, wielding a high-pressure hose. Not wanting our camera equipment soaked, we called our whale inspection crew back, hurriedly hauled the rubber boat up on deck, while Capt. Cormack crouched at the wheel, ready to dodge whichever way necessary to avoid being rammed, if that's what the Russians were up to.

Less than fifty yards from our port stern, the Soviet vessel veered off, and moved to the side of the dead whale. The Russians seemed in a tremendous hurry to get lines around its tail and lash it to the side of their ship. In their rush, they broke one line and snapped the jaw of the whale. It was a sickening sound.

From there, events moved with dizzying speed. We found a second dead sperm, this one slightly larger. The contrast between the magnificence of the live whales we had seen and the gray sluglike form floating before us now was so powerful that most of us became silent and grim-faced, each person sunk into his own thoughts. Few words were exchanged. Then the Russian harpoon boat swept toward us again. Choosing to move in through the rest of the fleet toward the *Dalniy Vostok*, we pulled away. The next two hours were spent churning steadily toward a gray silhouette on the horizon that loomed larger and larger until we were coming up on its stern just as two harpoon boats were bringing in their kills.

[*Text continues on page 44*]

Patrick Moore and cameraman Fred
   Easton approach the Russian factory
ship and two of its killer boats.

The *Dalniy Vostok* drags three dead sperm
whales through the water as two more
are taken up the stern slip to the
flensing deck.

Another whale for flensing

Two Greenpeace Zodiacs pursuing and
being pursued

Mike Bailey in the killer boat's line of
  fire

We dispatched two rubber boats which moved in between the harpoon boats, so close that the Russians gathered on the decks could yell questions. They didn't appear to know who we were or what we were doing. They didn't even appear to recognize the Canadian flag, although our United Nations flag seemed to draw their attention. Later we drew alongside the *Dalniy Vostok*, playing music to the crew through our four-foot-high loudspeakers. It was like driving slowly past an apartment complex.

The Russians gathered on the decks, looking down at us. Some waved. Some pretended to ignore us. Others stared expressionlessly. A few shook their fists and made gestures which translator Korotva told us meant something quite unprintable. The officers on the bridge, wearing traditional Russian black wool caps, observed us closely with binoculars. Using our sound system, Korotva told them that we were against the killing of whales, that we intended to try to prevent them from killing any more whales, and that we represented the fifty-two nations which voted at the United Nations for a ten-year moratorium on whaling. The Russians did not react noticeably to our message. Either they didn't understand or they were shrugging it off.

By midafternoon we were satisfied that we had documented the entire factory ship operation—the loading of the whales and the continuing methodical carnage on the deck, with great torn chunks of whale being hauled about on chains and shattered bones thrusting up like the wreckage of buses—and we picked out a harpoon boat, the *Vlastny, PK 2007*, waited until it had turned over half a dozen whales, and followed it as it set out on a new hunt.

The chase lasted until 7:30 P.M. It was a wild, wild ride. At one point we had three harpoon boats strung out halfway to the horizon ahead of us, with a fourth steaming up on our stern, veering to the side only after it had pulled up to within a few hundred feet of us, then sweeping past our port side at fifteen knots, passing within ten yards. Casually, as though toying with us, the Soviet crewman standing at the harpoon swung his weapon in our direction, aiming it directly at us, while others of the crew laughed and made more rude gestures. Everybody on board the Greenpeace ships had been instructed to avoid any threatening or abusive acts or behavior to avoid unnecessary provocation. Still, I heard at least two of our crewmen burst out with angry shouts.

The Soviet vessel then swung across our bow. The move could only be described as contemptuous. The ship then easily pulled away, leaving our slower-moving seiner in its wake. We were all out on deck, our bodies tense with the effort of straining forward, as though we might move the boat along faster by sheer effort of willpower.

"It's like that kid's nightmare of running in slow motion, trying to catch up with somebody, but you can't," remarked Carlie Trueman, expressing it perfectly.

Just when it seemed hopeless, we saw the *Vlastny*, now some four miles ahead, suddenly change course. Even though we had overcome the astronomical odds against finding the fleet in the first place, we were now faced with the brute physical reality that the whaling ship could travel at least twice as fast as we could. Our advisors' warnings of the futility of our venture loomed dreadfully. Our only hope now was that Paul Spong had not been speaking madness when he said we could count, finally, on help from the whales.

On the bow of each killer boat is kept a
250-pound explosive harpoon at the
ready.

And now it came. I remember clearly that the hair on my neck stood up and goosebumps ran over my body, for the whales had turned and were racing—a whole pod—directly toward us, dragging the Russian whaling boat along in their wake. The whales could have fled in any direction. That they chose to come directly to the protective flank of the *Phyllis Cormack* was too much of a coincidence. In that moment we were all seized by the overwhelming sensation that the miracle we had been seeking had now presented itself. There was a hush on our decks and a moment when several of us wanted to throw ourselves down on our knees, to pray, to thank God.

But the time had come to act, to live up to our pledge to offer our bodies as shields. We were ready. Dr. Moore, crewman Paul Watson, Korotva, photographer Rex Weyler, cameraman Fred Easton and I had been in our wetsuits all day, waiting. The rubber boats were inflated; the engines had been primed.

In a maneuvre we had been practising for two months, Captain Cormack virtually jammed on the brakes, we hurled the rubber boats over the stern, throwing in life jackets after them, and bounded from the deck one by one. In three minutes the first rubber boat was zipping away from the *Phyllis Cormack*.

Watson and I headed straight for the *Vlastny*, with Moore and Easton in the second boat. Korotva and Weyler were delayed several minutes by an outboard engine failure. Assisted by crewman Will Jackson, they switched engines in record time, and came pounding out across choppy waters to join us.

Closing in on the harpoon boat was definitely the most exhilarating and terrifying moment of my life. We could see the whales—sperms—blowing in unison as they broke wildly to the surface, their blowholes, as large as manhole covers, blasting out founts of spray. Their humps thrust like glittering black shoulders. Even when they were still half a mile ahead, with the shriek of the outboard engine cutting through my brain, I could still hear distinct, tremendous gasps coming from the creatures.

After about ten minutes of leaping across the waves, being bounced around in the rubber boat like ping-pong balls, Watson and I found ourselves pulling neck and neck with the Russian boat. The whales were still ahead and although we could clearly see the Soviet gunner poised at his harpoon (it was baby-blue colored) he had yet to fire.

A fleeing pod of sperm whales

The moment had come to pull ahead and cut in front of the Russian bow. Watson and I had been hanging on for dear life and had not even time to look at each other except to signal for turns. We now clutched each other's hands tightly for a moment. Then Watson guided us smoothly into position. While he kept his eyes ahead, watching for the whales lest we over-run them and be caught on their shoulders as they came crashing to the surface, I watched the rusty iron bow of the *Vlastny* rise and fall like a giant axe bit over Watson's shoulder.

At moments we were less than ten feet in front of the Russians. At other moments, we moved forty to fifty feet out, trying to keep ourselves directly in front of the gun, which the gunner was aiming this way and that as the ship swung from one course to another each time the whales broke surface in a new place. Then our engine went dead.

The fuel tank had bounced into the air, coming down on the hose feeding fuel to the engine. With a sputter, the engine died and the rubber boat instantly lost speed. And the *Vlastny* was coming up behind us at full speed.

All Watson said was: "OH-oh!"

All I said was: "I think we're going to have to jump, Paul."

The Russian vessel did not change course. Just as I was about to jump out of its way, the bow wave picked us up and lifted us sweetly away from the hull. The 150-foot ship passed so close I could have touched it. I looked up to see a power-fully-built bearded man standing beside the gunner, laughing as though it were a joke. Then the boat swept past us and Watson was clawing at our outboard while I pounded my fists against the side of our boat, swearing furiously.

The next thing I knew, our two other rubber boats had closed in, and George Korotva was yelling, "Get in! Get in!" I scrambled into his craft, cameraman Easton jumped in beside Watson, and we sped off in the two remaining boats.

We caught up with the Russians within minutes. By this time, they were plowing so close to the whales that their harpoon gun was actually being aimed downward.

I thought at the time there were only five or six whales in the pod, but observers back on the *Phyllis Cormack*, which had pulled up to the disabled rubber boat, established that there were in fact ten of them.

While Korotva and I darted back and forth in front of the harpoon boat, Moore and Weyler sped ahead until they were alongside the fleeing whales. The chase was taking place at about fifteen knots, with the whales surfacing every few minutes. When they blew, rainbows formed in the spray.

The sight was so beautiful and so horrifying, with the great killer boat driving down behind us, that for the first time tears leaped into my eyes and I was partially blinded for a moment.

That was when I heard the sound of the harpoon gun going off and the "whish" of the cable whipping out behind it. It slashed the water less than five feet from the port side of our rubber boat. The moment we heard the sound, Korotva and I instinctively ducked. By this time Watson had his engine running and had moved in on our starboard side with cameraman Easton, who caught the entire sequence on film. Our second cameraman, Ron Precious, recorded the confrontation from the bridge of the *Phyllis Cormack.*

We had been warned by whale experts about the dangers of being near a wounded animal. Their best advice was that after a whale had been shot we should stand well clear of the area, before an enraged bull took his anger out on the nearest target, most likely a small rubber boat and not a steel-hulled killer boat.

As we were speeding back toward *Phyllis Cormack,* no less than half a mile away, we could see behind us a bull rising up beside his mortally-wounded mate. He turned in a rush, but instead of heading toward us, he charged toward the killer boat. Casually, methodically, the gunner slacked off the line attached to the thrashing wounded female, reloaded, and blasted the bull down in the middle of his anguished, futile, attack.

Thoroughly shaken, we hauled ourselves up on to the *Phyllis Cormack* deck. Captain Cormack got underway and we headed toward the Russians with our cameras again aimed and loaded. From what we had seen so far, the Russian pattern seemed to be to get as many whales in a pod as possible and we could count about eight sperms fleeing toward the horizon, but the Russians seemed more concerned with lashing the two they had already killed to the side of their ship. At the same time they turned and started toward factory ship *Dalniy Vostok,* which had been steaming full speed toward us during the entire forty-minute confrontation. As far as we could tell, the eight surviving whales managed to get away—at least for one day more.

That night, we stayed close to the *Dalniy Vostok.* At dawn, we closed in within 100 yards. This time the Russians on deck neither smiled nor waved. Most of those who looked at us at all glared or made gestures, especially the crews on the chaser boats that pulled in with early-morning loads of dead whales. When one of the chaser boats set out, we started after it. After half a mile or so, seemingly uncertain about what to do, the boat changed course back toward the *Dalniy Vostok*. When it set out again, it did so at full speed, outrunning us.

We were at least four miles from any Soviet vessels all day. We were unable to get any closer. It seemed for several hours that they were not catching any whales at all, but at about 2:00 P.M., we came across another bloated gray sperm carcass with an antenna, radar reflector, and Russian flag attached. We thought that if we could not overtake the Russians, we could at least wait until they came to pick up the whale's corpse and then attempt to prevent them from recovering it. We waited until dark, and the Russians still had not arrived. By 11:00 P.M. we could see the lights of the *Dalniy Vostok* moving off across the horizon, so we left the dead whale and set out again at full speed.

It was Saturday night, June 28. The entire Soviet fleet (at least nine vessels, including the *Dalniy Vostok*) was in motion, heading far westward, then southward. We managed to stay in the midst of it until late at night and any observer in an aircraft would have assumed we were part of the fleet. We kept a triple watch on the lights all around us.

By Sunday morning the *Dalniy Vostok* had pulled several miles ahead of us and the harpoon boats were fanned out ahead of it, moving farther and farther away. We realized that we were crossing San Francisco's latitude and that we had been with the Russian fleet since we were due west of the California-Oregon border. This was not a direction we expected them to be taking, since it was so different from their hunts in previous years. At roughly 4:00 P.M. the factory ship—the last Russian vessel we could see—passed over the horizon and disappeared from our radar, still heading south.

By this time, we had at least two people on board with stomachaches from eating oil-soaked food and everyone was worn out and feeling sick. Taking stock of our supplies, we realized that we had been at sea nonstop for two weeks and that we were at the very end of our resources. The only course seemed to be to give up the chase temporarily and head into San Francisco, where Greenpeace had plenty of support from groups like Friends of the Earth, the Sierra Club, the Oceanic Society and Project Jonah, to take on fresh supplies and head out again.

We did not find the Russians again that year. After two more weeks of searching at sea, we finally had to conclude that they had moved out of our range. Eighty-five days after we left Vancouver, we returned. We had saved eight whales. And we were now $40,000 in debt.

If their aim is good, and the whale's flight
not swift enough . . .

The Second Year Begins

The fall, winter, and spring that followed became an organizational vortex that made the year which had passed seem casual. In addition to having to deal with financial problems, we also had to cope with the problems of success. A movie outfit from New York wanted to make a multi-million-dollar movie. Book contracts were offered. Lecture tours were arranged. Greenpeace groups sprang up from Tennessee to northern Saskatchewan. The horrors of administration fell full upon us. In the midst of it, several of our crew members decided they wanted to launch an expedition to the coast of Labrador in March to try to prevent the massacre of baby harp seals. And of course we wanted to mount an even larger and more effective expedition to interfere with the whale slaughter again.

To this end, we found that a new breed of people were willing to work with us: economists, lawyers, publishers, businessmen, bankers. We began to learn new skills, to come to grips with the magic of cash flow projections, budgets, payment schedules. We took on raffles, learned how to do computerized mail-outs, brochures, how to properly merchandise posters, T-shirts, buttons, trinkets. We were approached by every imaginable sort of hustler and entrepreneur, all trying to cash in on the publicity that had been generated by the Greenpeace name. It was both the most depressing and exhilarating period most of us had ever experienced, certainly the most exhausting.

The legal fees began to pile up too. In September, six of us were arrested and thrown in jail for trying to prevent the loading of a Soviet supply boat in Vancouver. In March, two helicopters we had chartered to take us to the Labrador ice packs to interfere with the seal hunt were seized by the R.C.M.P. and we were all charged with violating the Canadian Seal Protection Act. Our crime had been to try to protect the seals.

Yet somehow, by April 1976, we had managed to pay off the bills, cover the costs of the anti-sealing expedition, save

Bob Hunter returns a tattered banner to
the Kwakiutl Indians. Their traditional
motif has long graced Greenpeace's
flags and sails.

several hundred seals, get all our people back and, in the meantime, put some $50,000 worth of work into the *James Bay*, a retired Royal Canadian Navy minesweeper which we now proposed to take out into the North Pacific to tackle the whaling fleets again.

If the first antiwhaling expedition had been dominated by an almost religious obsession and a feeling of reverence and fear, the second expedition seemed to be colored by a mood that was far more corporate and even military. In this winter of 1975-76 we were guided more by cash flow projections than the *I Ching*. Most of the mystics had deserted us and financial advisors had moved in to fill the space. Moreover, we were not looking for a repeat of the miracle which had finally put us between the whales and the harpoons. Instead, we were looking for a full-fledged eco-guerrilla operation, wherein we would be able to match the speed and range of the whalers, and butt up against them shoulder-to-shoulder.

Music had been everywhere on the first trip and we had had more musicians among the crew than mechanics. Now, with a 153-foot converted minesweeper to run, we could not afford that ratio. We needed mechanics and music came second. There were many among us who lamented the fading of the old freewheeling roller-coaster that plunged blindly ahead on faith alone. Now we had a Board of Directors, a Board of Governors, committees by the score, a comfortable suite of poster- and plant-decorated offices, computers, a mailing list of 80,000 supporters, even an accounts payable department. Greenpeace had acquired the beginnings of a corporate technostructure. The spiritual people were slightly dismayed. But the more hardnosed among us were pleased, and the test, finally, would be whether we could do a better job than before. It remained that the whales probably did not care whether we saved them by chanting mantras on the deck or by plugging into a high-flying satellite, so long as we did it. But even though it had slipped into the background, the aura of mystery remained. The memories of those whales coming directly toward us out of the Pacific were fixed forever in our minds.

Above, Greenpeace's onshore
office in late 1975. Below, Amy
Ephron, agent for a New York
producer, bargains for movie
rights in the Greenpeace story.

Country Joe MacDonald sings to an
audience of 30,000 in Vancouver's
Jericho Park for the benefit of
Greenpeace.

Now to make the *James Bay* seaworthy . . .

Ron Marining, Walrus Oakenbough,
Mel Gregory, Bob Hunter, and Peter
Fruchman aboard the *James Bay*, tied
up beside the *Phyllis Cormack*

Kazumi Tanaka, photographer, poet,
Japanese translator

The *James Bay* sits under seizure by
Canadian customs near Bamfield,
B.C., leaving Walrus to his music.
Photograph by Noriko

Above, Paul Spong consults the
I Ching in his bunk. Left,
skipper George Korotva of the
James Bay

A 1976 rendezvous, 100 miles off Cape
Mendocino, at the site of the 1975
confrontation with the Russian whalers
(Photograph copyright 1976 by
Nicholas Wilson)

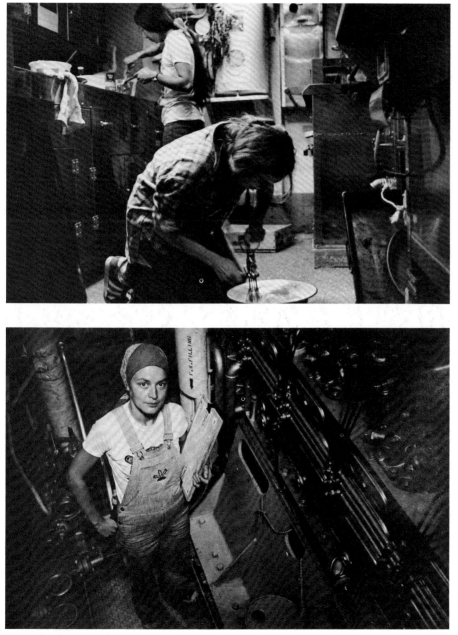

At work in the galley

Crewmember Bree Drummond

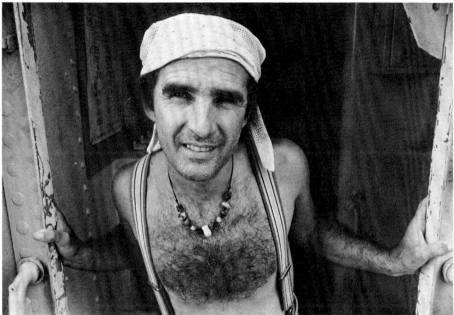

Barry Lavendar, artist and crewmember

Helmsman Lance Cowen, ex-U.S. Navy officer

Susi Leger, crewmember from Newfoundland

Gary Zimmerman, a San Francisco
oceanographer, standing watch in the
James Bay generator room

The *James Bay* on patrol

First Encounter, 1976

The second voyage to save the whales was launched from the site of the United Nations Conference on the Human Environment, with representatives of almost every country on earth standing by to see us off. Musicians such as Ronee Blakley and Country Joe MacDonald showed up to perform a benefit for us. A Cree Indian medicine man named Fred Mosquito appeared to proclaim us the long-awaited Warriors of the Rainbow. The day we left was the final day of an Earth-Healing ceremony conducted by native leaders from all over North America, with simultaneous services taking place in Findhorn (Scotland), Los Angeles, San Francisco, Palo Alto, Nigeria and Miami. The United Nations conference was extended two days so that the final day would coincide with the launching of our vessel. No more auspicious beginning could have been hoped for.

We were far better prepared and organized than we had been the previous year. With rainbows painted on its bow and seven Zodiac inflatable boats stored on the afterdeck, ready to be swung into the water on a moment's notice, our vessel was quickly dubbed a "mindsweeper." We had taken a quantum leap in terms of our actual capability between last year and this. Still, by the time we finally finished the work of overhauling and refitting the boat, raising money, and getting the equipment and people together, we were all completely exhausted. And the voyage had yet to begin.

The eighty-foot *Phyllis Cormack*, which had carried us to the Aleutian Islands and out into the midst of the Russian whaling fleet, seemed dwarfed by the *James Bay*. But she was traveling with us again, to take up a patrol along the West Coast while the larger vessel would attempt to move out into the real deeps of the Pacific.

Within less than two weeks from the time we set out, we realized we had scored an early victory. No whaling fleet came close to the West Coast, and, by then, the whalers had lost their chance to catch the sperm whales on their northward migration past the coast of California.

By July 12, it was clear the first stage of our offshore eco-patrol had served its function. In the course of it we had landed briefly at Portland, Oregon, and San Francisco. Now it was time for the smaller *Phyllis Cormack* to head back north, making one last sweep along the continental shelf, while the *James Bay* headed west from San Francisco. We had put a good part of our energy during the winter into establishing an intelligence network that would provide us with solid data on the movements of both the Japanese and Russian whaling fleets. Whether the network would work or not was something we could only find out by testing it. According to our information, the Russians by then were operating north of the Hawaiian Islands.

Almost immediately after clearing the Golden Gate Bridge we were hit by winds up to forty-five knots and swells that peaked at fourteen feet. The *James Bay* was narrow-beamed and tended to roll heavily, which left us after one night at sea with only ten people out of a crew of thirty capable of getting out of their bunks.

After two days of rough weather, the sea calmed. The Soviet fleet was reported whaling very close to Kauai, northwest of Oahu, which put them almost a month behind schedule in their operation off the West Coast. The Japanese fleet was still reported near Midway. Captain George Korotva set a course directly for the Russians.

By July 17, we were 1,100 miles from San Francisco. The Soviet fleet, according to our intelligence reports, was 500 miles directly ahead to the west. An inspection of our ship revealed that the starboard bow runner had been torn loose during the rough weather. Due to a late-night foul-up in radio communications from Vancouver, an inaccurate calculation of the position of the Soviet fleet was made, leaving the crew with the impression that the Russians were somewhere within fifty miles, even though electronics specialist Al Hewitt was unable to find a trace of any whalers on his radio direction finding equipment. Nor could a Russian voice be found on the whaling radio frequencies either. A full crew alert resulted in no sleep for anyone as we prepared Zodiacs in the dark and monitored every piece of the converted minesweeper's sophisticated tracking gear. Towards dawn, the expected interception point came and went without a trace of the Russian fleet.

The bleary-eyed crew had to live for close to a full day with the agonizing possibility that the Russians might have somehow slipped past in the night, and were now heading straight for North America, with Greenpeace too far out at sea to be able to turn around and give chase. Tempers flared in the morning. An exhausted communications and strategy team was unable to explain how, after a full year of preparations and groundwork, we had managed to go wrong. Morale dropped rapidly. Paranoia set in with amazing speed.

We had sent representatives to five different countries during the winter of 1975-76, searching for a foolproof method of finding the whaling fleets on the deep sea. We had sought out diplomats, bureaucrats, sympathizers in the employment of several governments, politicians and political aides, scientists and maritime authorities from literally hundreds of organizations. We had also systematically established contacts with conservation groups around the world, each with its own network of connections and friends in positions to have access to the highly secret information we wanted, namely, how to find the whalers in the middle of the North Pacific Ocean. In large part due to the coincidence that Vancouver had played host to the largest United Nations convention in history, at the very time that Greenpeace was preparing to launch a second expedition after the whaling fleets, this vital but incredibly elusive information was finally obtained. A world-wide intelligence network had been established to guide us across the vastness of the Pacific to the whaling fleets. Now, 1,100 miles west of North America, and in no position to make a complete return run, it looked as though our elaborate efforts had been in vain.

Having decided to hold a course according to our original calculations, despite the new but ultimately inaccurate information, we put out urgent calls to several world capitols, trying desperately to straighten out our intelligence data. It was not until noon that a coded message arrived from the Greenpeace headquarters in Vancouver confirming a "clerical error." We were still on the right course for an interception of the Russian fleet within twenty-four hours. They had not slipped past in the night.

In the early hours of the following morning, we picked up Russian voices over the radio. We quickly got an RDF fix, altered course slightly, and began zeroing in. There was a slight discrepency between our information and the radio signals, indicating that the Russians had altered their own course within the last day. They had dodged to the north, which suggested that they were indeed trying to slip past Greenpeace. It also seemed clear that the Russians had held back until now before moving toward North America.

We were close to our point of no return in terms of fuel. At dawn, the sky was gray. But by 7:00 A.M. it had started to clear ahead. Up on the flying bridge, Bob Thomas of Greenpeace Ottawa was the first to spot the distant shapes of the whaling boats. Crewman David Garrick wrote in his journal: "They are whaling. The same pattern as last year. A blast of smoke—turnabout and zig-zag in a grid system of search, and then blast away. The entire fleet is almost lazy in its appearance of 'hunting' on the horizon." It was the same fleet encountered the previous year—the *Dalniy Vostok* factory ship and nine 150-foot rusting steel killer boats with the harpoons mounted like cannons on the bow.

The *James Bay* seemed to sweep across the water toward the whalers, catching them in the middle of their operation. Immediately, their fleet started to break up, with killer boats heading off in every direction. One killer boat, *NK-2007*, started to head toward us. Then we saw the spouts in the water ahead of the vessel. "Whales!" The whales again were coming straight toward us, bringing the Russians along behind. Immediately, the *James Bay* stopped and three Zodiacs were hurled over the side. In the first Zodiac, Paul Spong took the controls, with my wife Bobbi and me riding in front. Two other Zodiacs swung in behind the lead boat, cameras clicking and whirring. Within minutes, we had successfully moved into position directly in front of the racing *NK-2007*. The man at the harpoon was crouched low, the harpoon swinging this way and that, and for at least ten minutes, it looked as though the Russians were intent on firing the harpoon as they did before, regardless of the risk to three human beings in the way. But suddenly, to everyone's relief and amazement, the gunner stepped back, flipped open the bolt, and the harpoon clicked downward. The *NK-2007* gradually came to a complete halt in the water. By this time there were four Greenpeace Zodiacs in front of it, four tiny rubber speedboats which had brought a huge metal killing machine to a dead stop. In the meantime, to the accompaniment of cheers from the *James Bay*, the pod of whales which had been desperately fleeing the Russian ships now swam swiftly over the horizon.

On the *NK-2007*, the Russians meanwhile slipped a canvas cover over the harpoon in an almost pathetic effort to hide the weapon from the probing cameras. Once we were satisfied that the pod of whales which was being hunted was now safe, the Zodiacs returned to the *James Bay*, and Captain Korotva spun the wheel, taking us rapidly across the water toward the *Dalniy Vostok* itself. In his journal, David Garrick noted: "No whales were killed this morning by *NK-2007*." Pulling up within 500 feet of the starboard side of the gigantic factory ship, the *James Bay* easily matched the Russian vessel's speed, while two more Zodiacs were dropped into the water to take cameramen right up to the stern of the *Dalniy Vostok* to document the transfer of dead whales from the killer boats to the factory ship. Our crew carried out the operation swiftly, for fear that the killer boats might scatter as soon as possible.

Paul Watson drove his Zodiac right up onto the back of a dead whale, hoping that the Russians would stop the loading operation. Instead, they continued hauling the dead whale up into the slipway at the stern, with the result that Watson's Zodiac was lifted almost four feet out of the water before it slipped off the back of the whale into the churning turbulence immediately behind the propellers of the massive factory ship. The Zodiac came very close to capsizing and photographer Matt Herron lost $2,000 worth of camera equipment. Japanese interpreter Kazumi Tanaka was almost dumped.

A Greenpeace Zodiac crew films the
Dalniy Vostok, a killer boat, and their
load of whales.

Paul Watson and Marilyn Kaga
position their boat between the
Russians and the fleeing whales.

A Russian harpooner and crew at the gun
of a halted killer boat

A Greenpeace Zodiac, with the *James Bay*
between two harpoon boats

Above, Russian crew members awaiting the next move. Below, George Korotva, Susi Leger, and Paul Spong in the *James Bay* wheelhouse

Eileen Chivers passes whale buttons and
an antiwhaling message to a harpoon
boat crewmember.

The *James Bay* and a Russian harpoon boat

Cameraman Fred Easton after his
encounter with the Russians

The last journey for two sperms

We Turn Back

After that, the *James Bay* cruised beside the *Dalniy Vostok* while the crew members appealed to the Russians in six languages—English, French, Russian, Japanese, Spanish and Czechoslovakian—to stop whaling immediately. Obviously disturbed by the impact this might be making on his crew, the captain of the *Dalniy Vostok* spurred his huge vessel to a top speed of eighteen knots, bearing due north. Until the moment we arrived on the scene, the Russians had been heading east. Now, they changed course, moving in a direction that took us farther by the minute from the nearest possible refueling point in Honolulu. It was clear that the Soviet captain wanted to test our ability to keep up with him. Captain Korotva accepted the challenge, and the *James Bay* leaped forward, pulling steadily ahead of the *Dalniy Vostok*. All the other Russian boats had disappeared entirely. Only the *Dalniy Vostok* and the *James Bay* remained racing each other across the water. The race went into the night, and our crew had the dizzying experience, perhaps unique, of being a lone unarmed vessel actually chasing a fleet of ships across the ocean. The camera had somehow become more powerful than the cannon.

After a forty-hour top-speed pursuit of the Russians northward, we reached the point of no return for our fuel supply. The forty-hour interruption of the whaling operation had cost the Russians more than ten times as much. Moreover, during that period they had not been able to slow down to carry out their routine hunting operation. We estimated that this single encounter had cost the Russians roughly 50,000 gallons of diesel fuel. And for each whale they failed to kill, they lost $20,000. "We have hurt them, no doubt about it," said Dr. Spong. There were believed to have been at least five whales in the pod which was directly saved by Greenpeace intervention, representing a total value to the whalers of $100,000. At 11:00 P.M., July 20, the *James Bay* was forced to drop back from the still-fleeing Russian fleet. We turned toward Honolulu, with just enough fuel remaining to make landfall.

The next day a sperm whale surfaced half a mile ahead of us, just as the huge speakers on the boat were blaring out music across the ocean. A pod, including a baby, appeared. There were at least five of them. This was the first time we had seen live sperm whales, other than those in the process of being hunted. Dr. Spong speculated that this particular pod could well be the one we had saved earlier. Certainly this particular group of sperms (the whales with the most highly developed brains of all the *cetacea*) was responding directly to the music and the reactions of the crew.

For close to an hour, the whale family breached and blew around the bow of the *James Bay* and the celebration might have gone on for a long time but for the fact that no more fuel could be spared. Had Greenpeace not appeared, these whales would undoubtedly have become shoe polish or lubricating oil, possibly in a Soviet ICBM. At one point, just before the *James Bay* had to veer away toward the fuel pumps at Honolulu, the entire pod came to a halt, waiting, allowing us to glide right into their midst. Several great heads loomed above the water, peering at us. A sudden unexpected squall came up, soaking the crew. Then the whales sounded and were gone. The entire crew was ecstatic, singing songs all night. In the morning we awoke to find ourselves sailing directly into the largest, clearest, double-ringed rainbow that any crew member could ever remember seeing.

The *James Bay* off the coast of Maui

The crew of the *James Bay* in Honolulu

More Waiting . . .

The first reconnaissance flight out to French Frigate Shoal had to be aborted when the U.S. Navy ordered the aircraft out of the area because of missile tests taking place. An elaborate scheme, involving sending five Greenpeacers out on aerial reconnaissance flights in every direction from the Hawaiian Islands, was devised. Other Greenpeacers, including Japanese interpreters Taeko Miwa and Kazumi Tanaka, set out to visit virtually every Japanese vessel in Honolulu, managing to obtain from their countrymen the radio frequencies for the Japanese whaling boats. We systematically contacted every sympathetic politician available, as well as making personal contacts with U.S. Air Force, Navy and Coast Guard personnel. At the official level, Greenpeace got no assistance. Unofficially, many individuals, both civilian and military, agreed to help.

Within hours of arriving in Honolulu, we were inundated by the arrival of hundreds of supporters. Good press coverage and appeals over the radio soon resulted in a steady trek of Hawaiians bringing food to the boat. We quickly discovered there was a powerful sentiment running against whaling among the Hawaiian islanders. Support came from every level: The harbormaster waived moorage fees. The mayor's office sent its greetings. And the U.S. Coast Guard reported that a Japanese whaling fleet had been spotted near French Frigate Shoal at the leeward Hawaiian Islands.

We now faced an exquisite dilemma. Immediately after the *James Bay* was forced to fall back for fuel, the Soviets altered their northward course and headed due east toward the continent. The *Kyokuyo Maru #3* Japanese whaling fleet was reported to have immediately pulled away from French Frigate Shoal the moment its presence was reported in the press. Its exact location was a mystery. We had to choose between heading back toward North America after the Russians, or plunging westward after the Japanese. We decided to maintain a position in Honolulu until hard data could be obtained on the Japanese fleet's position. To this end, we established contact with several Hawaiian supporters who had aircraft at their disposal. [*Text continues on page 86*]

Fred Easton at Midway Island Naval Station

On board a Coast Guard flight from
Honolulu to Midway Island, searching
for the Japanese whaling fleet

On July 30, we departed from Honolulu, moving northward toward the Japanese fleet. Four crew members remained behind to continue aerial reconnaissance. The plan was to move our ship to the island of Kauai, where it could remain, without consuming fuel, until definite word came back from the reconnaissance crew. Putting in at the small port of Nawiliwili, Greenpeace was now about 200 miles closer to the last known position of the Japanese while continuing to monitor, via our intelligence network, the movement of the Russians. It had now become clear that the Soviet fleet was not proceeding on its usual course to the California coast. Instead, it had stopped short, some 800 miles from North America, unwilling to risk further exposure.

While the *James Bay* and its crew waited impatiently in Nawiliwili, the reconnaissance team succeeded in arranging to fly over roughly 170,000 square miles of ocean around the Hawaiian Islands, easily the largest aerial ecology action ever undertaken. They flew north, south, and west as far as the remote island of Midway. At the end of six intensive days of searching, the reconnaissance crew joined us in Nawiliwili. They reported no trace of the Japanese fleet, indicating that the *Kyokuyo Maru #3* had pulled far back from Hawaii. A report from Honolulu told us that the U.S. ambassador had had a quiet talk with the Japanese ambassador, advising him that it would be unfortunate for U.S.-Japanese relations if a confrontation with environmentalists were to occur so close to American territorial waters. Not only was the whaling fleet asked to withdraw, but all Japanese fishing boats moved off as well.

When we were satisfied that the Japanese fleet had moved to the west, the *James Bay* steamed from Nawiliwili to take up a position at Lahaina, a port on the island of Maui. By this time, the Russians had started to retreat across the Pacific, having avoided the entire coastal area of North America for the first time since modern whaling began. It was still too early for us to move directly out to sea, since the Russians were so far away that we would not have the necessary fuel to conduct a proper confrontation.

Al Hewitt, engineer and electrician

The pressure of waiting took its toll. And since we had been so long kept from making any decisive move, the crew was more than frustrated. Everyone was both physically and psychologically exhausted. An unusual heat wave had gripped the Hawaiian Islands for weeks, and in the heat the crew, most of it Canadian, was also suffering from heat exhaustion. Tempers were ragged. Accustomed to rushing at breakneck speed, the crew was unprepared for a protracted period of intelligence-gathering, reconnaissance, and patient waiting for the right moment to move out. Tensions grew, dissolved, grew again, dissolved again. At least half of the crew was suffering from dehydration. In our time at sea we had been thoroughly banged about in the metal interior of the *James Bay* and in the sweltering tropical heat, even the smallest cut quickly became infected, which kept our nurse, Marilyn Kaga, very busy indeed. Crew morale was dangerously low, almost to the point where it looked like the expedition might not be able to continue.

At last, refueled and resupplied by Maui residents, we moved out to confront the Soviet fleet, which had begun to cross back over the Pacific in a direction that would take them north of the Hawaiian Islands. Less than three hours out of Lahaina, however, an accident occurred. The youngest crew member on board, twenty-year-old David Weiss, of Woodstock, New York, got his finger caught in a rope attached to a bucket tossed into the water as the vessel moved along at eleven knots. One-third of the fourth finger on his right hand was literally ripped away. Because of his belief in organic foods and healing methods, David refused to take any painkillers or sedatives. Captain Korotva wheeled the boat around and raced back to Lahaina, where a U.S. Coast Guard ambulance was waiting. We decided to wait another day in Lahaina to make sure David's injury was properly taken care of.

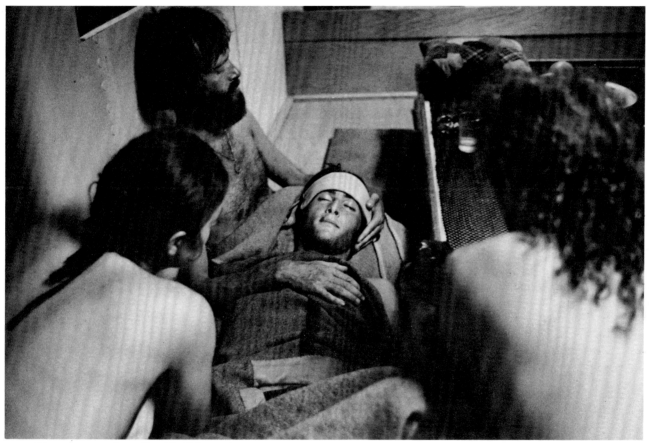

The crew comforts David Weiss, who
lost a finger in a deck accident.

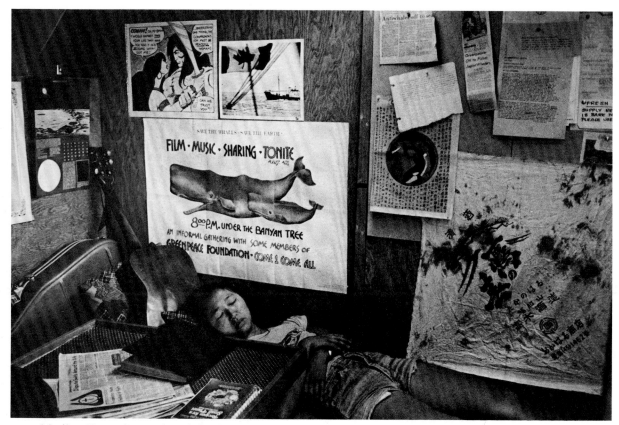

Marilyn Kaga sleeps aboard the *James Bay*.

To Sea Again

Now we needed fresh water and, unable to get it in Lahaina, the *James Bay* moved the following day down the coast of Maui to the port of Kahului. From there we set out, heading due north on a course which would intercept the returning *Dalniy Vostok* within a week. By now, our crew—once numbering thirty-one—was down to twenty-seven, on a vessel which in wartime carried a crew of forty. As though to compound the feeling that our luck had almost run out, we awoke that night to find a fire blazing in one of the bunkrooms. It was quickly put out, but not before the entire main deck was blanketed in smoke. Camera equipment worth several thousand dollars came close to being ruined.

By August 11, the Russian fleet was estimated to be 1,300 miles away, slightly west of the anticipated interception point. On the afterdeck an electric circuit blew out, producing lightninglike blue flashes and a fire between two fuel drums. It too was quickly put out. By this time, with a string of injuries and two fires behind us, the crew was becoming truly jittery. Fire drills, man-overboard drills, and abandon-ship drills were repeated several times to freshen the crew's readiness for any disaster.

We entered a heavy fog bank on August 12. Crewman Hal Ward was on watch when, to his surprise, he spotted a blip on the radar, even though we were well off the normal shipping lanes. The blip indicated some kind of craft four miles off the port bow. When the fog lifted temporarily, Ward was able to make out, with binoculars, a low, dark, rectangular shape against the gray mist. Its running lights suddenly came on and the strange craft began to move away. Captain Korotva reported later that it was definitely a submarine. The only question was: *whose* submarine?

Abruptly, the blip vanished from the radar screen, indicating that the sub had gone below the surface. The submarine was to haunt us for the next week, appearing and reappearing, never coming any closer (on the surface) than four miles. The crew became acutely aware of its presence, not knowing whether to view it as a guardian angel or—more ominously—as a military craft sent by the Russians to protect their whaling interests. This added to our sense of vulnerability on the unarmed *James Bay*, a feeling not lessened by the fact that radio communications with land could successfully take place only during the night. This meant that if someone did make a move against us during the day, we would be unable to get even a last-minute report out.

To be out this far in the middle of the North Pacific, the submarine, we thought, would likely be nuclear-powered. Its presence had a subtle psychological impact on the crew, creating a feeling of wariness, a sense of our actual weakness relative to the might of the two major superpowers. It gave us back the sensations that ancient mariners must have lived through, knowing that out there in the vastness around them, under the water somewhere, gigantic monsters lurked. This one, evidently, had some interest in us. Whether its interest was simply to observe or whether it was to be used ultimately to "protect" the whaling fleet, was something none of us could say. We could only focus on the task at hand—to catch up to the whalers—and we closed the ominous thought of the submarine out of our minds, except to joke about it.

It was not until shortly after midnight, August 20, that we picked up a blip on the screen which did not subsequently vanish. From its shape, size, and speed, we judged it to be one of the Russian killer boats. It was drawing toward us at fourteen knots, eight miles dead ahead. As we continued our approach, the boat changed course and moved away. The consequences for us in lost fuel to engage in a full-speed chase now would have been disastrous. After half an hour, Captain Korotva throttled down the engines and went back to the charts, guessing that the vessel may have been at the forward fringe of the fleet, which he realized was moving back toward the place where we had been two days earlier. "They are working *around* us," he said. Judging from the radio signals, the fleet was spread out ahead of us in a fan shape. By dawn, fog had set in again.

We idled, carefully monitoring our radar and direction finder for any sign that the fleet might be changing its direction. At 10:40 in the morning, Captain Korotva said: "It's now or never. *Vostok* is dead ahead, maybe just over the horizon." The *James Bay* surged ahead at fourteen knots, striking for the center of the fleet. As we cleaved the fog and the waves, bits of plastic and garbage in the water appeared more frequently. More albatross appeared around us. Soviet voices crackled and jabbered through the loudspeakers, seemingly coming from every side. By noon the fog began to lift. We could see 300 yards, half a mile, a mile! There was still nothing on the radar. "Damn it, open her up," roared the captain. "They're just ahead! I *know* it!"

At 1:30 P.M. the first blip appeared on the radar, dead ahead. Five minutes later, a second blip, then a third, a fourth! "We've got them!" shouted helmsman Lance Cowan. By then, the *James Bay* was crashing through the water, bucking

Bob Hunter, Pat Moore, and navigator
Matt Herron consider the proper
strategy as we pursue the Russian
fleet through the fog.

and rolling. Zodiacs were readied and their outboard engines were tested. By then all ten Russian vessels were visible on radar. But it was still not until 5:30 that Bob Thomas—who had been first to spot the Soviets during the previous encounter —shouted from the flying bridge: "Dead ahead! I see them!" As we closed in, the fog—which had retreated to the horizon, giving us a brief ray-blast of sunlight—now also began to close in.

By 5:50, the *James Bay* came rapidly into the midst of a bizarre and unexpected scene. There was the mighty *Dalniy Vostok* on the horizon, a blunt gray shape. On our port bow, less than a mile away, eight killer boats were speeding one after the other in a circle, like horses on a weird merry-go-round, around a single killer boat at the center of the circle. Either the Russians were driving some whales into the center using an ultrasonic underwater sound screen or they were deliberately trying to prevent the *James Bay* from approaching the ship in the center without risking a near-certain collision. "They might be trying to hide a dead undersized whale in there," speculated Dr. Spong. We came to a dead stop, and two Zodiacs, equipped with radios, were quickly lowered. Dr. Spong took one Zodiac himself, along with photographer Rex Weyler and crewmember Susi Leger of Grand Falls, Newfoundland. Dr. Patrick Moore took a second craft with two other crewmen. Within moments, the two small craft were zipping over the waves toward the center of the circle of killer boats, easily dodging between them.

No sooner had the rubber boats left than Captain Korotva, stationed on the bridge, saw that the gray outline of the *Dalniy Vostok* had vanished entirely and that the most distant killer boat, perhaps three miles away from us, was rapidly turning into a mere shadow. The fog was rolling back in—swiftly! He immediately radioed the order to the rubber boats to return. "This is a command," he bellowed. "Return to *James Bay*! Return to *James Bay*! The fog is thick!" The radio in Dr. Spong's Zodiac was working, but there was no response from the other faster-moving craft, which had taken the lead and was streaking toward the central killer boat, its occupants too low in the water to be aware of the on-rolling shroud of fog. Dr. Spong's boat heard the command to return, but he could see and hear that the radio on the boat ahead was not working. Dr. Moore and his two companions were racing straight into a fog bank, unaware.

Paul Spong radios Vancouver while
   Greenpeace hunts.

Into a fog bank, unaware . . .

Pat Moore chases a Russian harpoon boat
through thick fog.

The Russians harpoon boat appears.

The Russians lash a sperm whale
to the side of their boat.

A Close Call

"We heard the skipper telling us to come back, but we had to catch up to the other guys to let them know, otherwise they'd end up alone, without a radio, in the middle of a fog in the middle of the Pacific Ocean." Dr. Spong's heavily-loaded Zodiac was unable, however, to catch up to Dr. Moore's boat. By then it was too late.

From the bridge of the *James Bay*, there was suddenly nothing to be seen but blankness. It was as though, earlier, a curtain had lifted on a tremendous stage, with Russian ships moving rapidly around in a circle. Our people had jumped in their boats and raced out onto the stage. And then the curtain came down and they were all swallowed up: Russian ships, dead whales, and six Greenpeacers.

The radio equipment in the rubber boats was, of course, about the cheapest money could buy, for there had been, as usual, almost no money to spare. For nearly two hours, the *James Bay* sought desperately to grope toward her lost children. To compound every problem, darkness was falling rapidly. On board the rubber boats, a series of hair-raising decisions had to be made on the spot. When at last the Zodiacs found each other, their dilemma became clear. The best move seemed to be to stay with the killer ship, for while the rubber boats were too small to be picked up on radar in the fog, the *James Bay* could at least track the killer boats themselves. Unfortunately, the "dead" killer boat—which had indeed been in the process of lashing what looked to be an undersized whale to its side, immediately fired up its engines and began moving at fourteen knots. The only hope for the crews on the rubber boats was to run with the killer boat, following in its wake.

That worked for over half an hour, but darkness was falling, the sea was picking up, and the occupants of the boats were taking a furious pounding. Worse, Dr. Spong's Zodiac steadily began to lose way, falling back foot by foot. The other craft easily kept pace, but had to keep falling back itself so as not to lose track of the Greenpeacers trailing behind. Finally, the thin visual link between the two rubber boats got stretched too far. Gasping from the pounding she was taking in the Zodiac, Susi Leger was forced to report: "We've lost them. Can't see them at all. We cut the engines. We've stopped . . . trying to figure out what to do."

Back on the *James Bay*, the anxiety level had now reached its peak. And the *James Bay* was having its own troubles, dodging the Russian killer boats that had doubled back and loomed suddenly out of the fog, one of them sweeping across our bow less than 100 feet ahead. The whole fleet was in chaotic motion, and it was impossible to tell on the radar which of the blips might be the one with the Greenpeace speedboat racing along behind. There was no indication at all where Dr. Spong and his crew might be. The Soviet fleet was straightening out its direction, moving in unison at full speed away from the scene. A very tense five minutes passed before Ms. Leger was able to radio: "We've found them! We're together!"

Greenpeace Zodiacs, hidden behind a
curtain of fog

Keeping his wits about him, Dr. Moore had spun his boat around 180 degrees at the moment he became aware that the Zodiac had vanished behind—immediately giving up the idea of following the Russian ship any farther—and tracked his way back to a pinpoint connection with the one remaining radio-equipped boat. Now, with the *James Bay* befogged and its two speedboats still in the water, it came down to their groping their way back together across whatever distance separated them, in whatever direction they might lie in relation to one another. Digging out a shortwave radio on his Zodiac, Dr. Spong worked out a careful signal system with the radio on board the mother ship. Captain Korotva crossed his fingers in the hope that the lost Greenpeacers would not prove to be out of range and began sending timed impulses.

There was no response at first. And then, finally, Dr. Spong picked up a trace of an impulse, zeroed in on it, and began the hour-long job of following the faint impulse back to the minesweeper. It began to rain. The darkness thickened. Then, shortly after what should have been sunset, a pale spike of light broke through from the west and the fog drew back almost a mile. Regular blasts of the *James Bay* foghorn had not been heard by the crews on the rubber boats, until finally Ms. Leger could yell joyously from the Zodiac: "We hear you! We hear you!" It was still another half hour before the bow waves of the rubber boats could be seen emerging from the fog. In their sojourn, the boats had gotten as far as five miles from the *James Bay.* Had they not found their way back by darkness, they might have drifted twenty or more miles away before dawn.

The *James Bay* emerges at last.

Last Meeting

Once the six soaking, shivering, exhausted Greenpeacers were safely back on board, the *James Bay* swung around and headed back after the fleet, the stragglers of which could still be seen on radar. Late that night, having caught up with the fleet again, Captain Korotva reported that our submarine "tail" had surfaced briefly just before we first found the whalers, and had surfaced for several minutes immediately after we began chasing them again, still astern of us.

"It was the size of a big ship," he reported. "Five miles aft at first. Then gone." That night, our radar suddenly went fuzzy. Sweeping patterns of dots appeared. Our radios and RDF equipment began acting up. Dr. Moore announced that we were being scanned by a very powerful radar, much more powerful than anything they had used on us from the *Vostok*.

By 6:30 the next morning, the *Dalniy Vostok* was six miles ahead, moving slowly at perhaps three to four knots. All of the killer boats had disappeared. The fog had cleared completely. The *Dalniy Vostok* was bearing northeast of us. We were now 1,500 miles from Hawaii. At 10:00 A.M. two killer boats appeared on our starboard beam. Through our binoculars, we saw that they were moving purposefully. "They're on whales!" We altered course immediately and came to full speed, bearing down on them, with all hands on deck. This time, we were prepared to try a double operation—stopping two killer boats at once. From the bridge someone shouted, almost screamed: "Hurry! I can see spouts! Whales! They're right on top of them!"

A shivery kind of feeling came over the crew. Everyone performed with spectacular efficiency. There were no foul-ups, no last-minute delays, no bungling, and no amateurish confusion. The *James Bay* came to an abrupt stop two miles from the point where the hunt was taking place. In less than a minute, the first Zodiac was in the water, piloted by Mike Bailey, with photographer Matt Herron and myself in the bow acting as radio operator. We fairly whistled toward the nearest killer boat. Within less than another minute, a second Zodiac was in the water, with Dr. Spong at the throttle and two crewmen. Dr. Spong and crew immediately set out to intercept the second killer boat, apparently also on whales. Before either Zodiac could close very much of the distance between themselves and their respective targets, a third speedboat was also in motion across the waves, piloted by Dr. Moore. But the whole beautiful maneuver came perhaps two minutes too late to save at least one whale. The harpoon cannon bloomed with white smoke. A whale died just ahead.

By the time the Zodiac driven by Bailey came rocketing up to the killer boat, the hulking, rusty ship was already stopped. In the water on its starboard side there was a tremendous thrashing and hard thunking, like a huge truncheon. "It's right in front of us," I radioed. "Blood all over the place, maybe two hundred feet around . . . the whale is still alive. It's smashing its tail against the side of the boat . . . you can see the harpoon sticking out . . . they've got a loop around the tail now . . ." The killer boat immediately took off, dragging the whale like a great sack at its side, except that the "sack" still flipped about, now rigid, now spastic. I couldn't tell whether it was still really alive when they started dragging it or not. But it certainly had been alive when we arrived, and it wasn't minutes later that they had it lashed and were underway. Three men at the bow of the vessel had already loaded another

A Greenpeace crew takes its last message
to the Russians: "Nyet!"—"Stop
killing the whales!"

harpoon in the gun. Bailey pushed his Zodiac until the wooden floor panels began to buckle from the pounding of the waves and then swerved in front of the Russians. Within less than five minutes, the harpooner stepped back from his weapon and began closing it down and binding it to the deck with restraining lines.

Now, instead of stopping, the killer boat sped up and began racing toward the *Dalniy Vostok*, which had changed course and was moving swiftly forward. From the flying bridge of the *James Bay*, observers could see the survivors of the whale pod moving steadily in the opposite direction. No one had time to do an accurate count, with attention fixed on three scattered Zodiacs and two killer boats. The consensus was that from five to eight surviving whales were spotted after the Russians decided to grab their one prize and run for the factory ship, like a dog grabbing a bone between its teeth and scrambling for a place to chew on it.

The second Zodiac operation proved to be more successful than the first. Dr. Spong and his crew reached their target before it could bloody even a single whale. The moment the Greenpeace Zodiac arrived, the killer boat revved up to top speed and steered southward toward the horizon. The Zodiac pursued them for six miles before turning back. Someone joked later: "It was like watching three little puppies come out to chase two huge wolves away from a herd of lambs."

While the *James Bay* stopped to pick up its slightly-bruised speedboat crew, the *Dalniy Vostok* moved at sixteen knots to the northeast—exactly the same tactic used by the Russians

during the previous encounter, namely, to move away from the nearest refueling point, knowing we would have to fall back sooner or later for lack of fuel.

Captain Korotva reported that at 1:50 P.M., while we were closing in on the *Dalniy Vostok*, our "unidentified blip" appeared suddenly on the radar, four miles off our port stern. It remained on the surface for only a minute and then was gone.

Captain Korotva gave the *James Bay* one last push. We ran hard for two hours. And then the word came from the chief engineer that we had just reached our point of no return. We immediately shut down the engines. At a strategy meeting that night we explored a series of possible actions; one of the more radical was that unless the Russians intended to go all the way back to North America, they must, at some point, decide to come back this way, giving us a chance to hit them as they ran. We had left Hawaii with a two-week food supply. We were in the twelfth day of our mission and faced a six-day return trip to the islands. But we decided to sit tight and maintain radio silence, again in the hope that the fleet, thinking we were gone, might come back into this area to hunt.

At 1:00 A.M., the mysterious blip appeared again on the radar. It remained for close to half an hour, dead in the water, eleven miles south of us. Then it vanished. This proved to be our last glimpse of "X," and we were left, finally, not knowing either the submarine's origins or its mission, or indeed anything else about it (other than the fact that it had been tailing us on and off for ten days). Our struggle with the

A Russian crew observes . . .

Russian whaling fleet had not gone unobserved, but it was impossible to say whether the observations had gone back to the Pentagon or the Kremlin. By breakfast time we reached a decision: we would go to Midway, refuel, and come back out. Dr. Spong calculated that the Russians would continue to hunt in this approximate area and that we had a very good chance of hitting them again. We began calling Vancouver to start to make the complex arrangements which had to be made if we were to be allowed entry to a strategic U.S. military base.

It was expected to take us six days to reach Midway, barring bad weather. For one full day we moved in this direction, confident that the Russian fleet—last seen proceeding northwest—would soon turn and zigzag its way back in the direction in which we were now moving. Water, already on strict ration, now went on doubly-strict ration and our staple foods were just about gone.

But on August 23, word came from Vancouver that the Russians, contrary to our expectations, had entirely abandoned the area north of the Hawaiian Islands. Instead, inexplicably, the *Dalniy Vostok* fleet was continuing on a steady northeast course, as though heading directly toward the Canadian west coast. Poring over records of past whale fleet movements, Dr. Spong concluded that, rather than sweeping back along the Hawaiian chain, as we had expected, the Soviets might in fact be planning a sweep along the Canadian coast and out through Alaskan waters to the Aleutian Islands. Not only was the *Dalniy Vostok* heading toward the Pacific northwest coast, but the entire fleet was moving so rapidly that it could only be engaged in sporadic whaling at the most. A 650-mile gap was already lying open between us.

Captain Korotva again cut the engines and another—it seemed like the ten thousandth—emergency strategy meeting was held. The problem came down to this: if, indeed, the Russians were heading north to Alaskan waters, it would be all but impossible to strike them again from Midway. We had the range to reach the Aleutians easily enough, but Greenpeace veterans from the 1971 voyage to oppose nuclear tests at Amchitka Island knew perfectly well that those waters are the most treacherous in the world and that the weather is beyond predicting. Chief Engineer Ted Hagarty, who had served on military vessels in that area, was also reluctant to push northward. He too saw that by the time the *James Bay* could refuel at Midway and move up to the Aleutians, the early autumn storms would likely have started.

Navigator Matt Herron furiously plotted alternative courses, and discovered that we were at a point in the North Pacific equidistant from four possible refueling spots, give or take ninety miles: Dutch Harbor in the mid-Aleutians; Midway; Honolulu; and, just barely, Winter Harbour on the west coast of Vancouver Island. Winter Harbour had not been considered earlier until Herron tried plotting a great circle route and discovered that, barring any kind of bad weather, we could still make the Canadian coast, but with virtually no margin of fuel left over. And by taking this route we would at least be hard on the heels of the *Dalniy Vostok*, and should she turn at any stage we had a good chance of interception.

We still had our food and other supplies to consider. The crew was advised of the situation and a decision was reached even though it meant that they would all tighten their belts even more than they had already been tightened. After one more check with Vancouver to make sure the Soviet fleet was still maintaining its northeast course back across the Pacific, Captain Korotva reversed course and we began moving toward North America instead of Midway.

By the next day the *Dalniy Vostok* slowed to nine knots, still moving on a northeast course which had already taken the Russians to within 1,000 miles of the coast of Oregon. Several stops and starts, while the *James Bay* had been moving steadily in their wake, reduced the distance between us to one full day's steaming. Meanwhile, we passed our point of no return for both Midway and Honolulu. It was now Vancouver Island or bust. Weather conditions changed almost from the moment we began moving northeastward. We picked up a following sea, with ten- and twelve-foot waves heaving themselves at our stern. This made for an uncomfortable trip but we were able to make good time and expend less fuel than we had estimated. We thus had a slight margin for another thrust at the whaling fleet should it come with range.

We were astonished to get word from Vancouver that three Soviet warships, including a 431-foot destroyer, had arrived in our home city for a "goodwill visit," the first such display of Russian military strength to make an appearance in any Canadian port since 1917. The coincidence was awesome. At a press conference in Vancouver, the following story came out: The chargé d'affaires of the Ottawa Soviet embassy was on hand, along with Russian Rear Admiral V. F. Barkanov. The first question for the Admiral was whether he had heard of the Greenpeace Foundation. He replied that, yes, he had and he understood that it was "a very responsible group." Asked what he thought about Greenpeace's efforts to halt whaling, the Soviet chargé d'affaires announced that Russia "will stop whaling within one or two years."

Dumbfounded but elated, the crew of the *James Bay* broke out two precious bottles of wine and celebrated. A message was sent from the boat: "If reports from Vancouver are true, that the Russian whaling fleet will be dismantled within two years, then we, the crew of the *Greenpeace VII*, can only rejoice . . ."

But we were not allowed to rejoice for long. Promptly the next morning came a report from the Associated Press in Moscow quoting a "highly-placed source in the Soviet Ministry of Fisheries," denying that Russia had any intention of stopping the whale slaughter. The source added: "The Soviet Union probably won't be doing much whaling by 1980, because of the diminishing whale populations." There, in a single bold stroke, Russia's true intentions toward the whales were laid bare. After years of pretending to observe International Whaling Commission quotas, of paying lip service to the concept of "sustainable yield," of talking loftily about "harvesting," the truth was finally flushed into the open. Russia planned to continue to slaughter the whales until there were not enough left to make it worth the bother. Greenpeace's tone turned sharply from praise to renewed outrage. The crew sent out a statement: "What this reveals about so-called 'progressive' Soviet thinking is that the Kremlin's attitude toward ecology is at the level of environmental Stalinism. It looks like the Gulag Archipelago for the whales."

That same day, the Russian fleet veered slightly eastward, as though it planned to head in close to the American west coast, but by nightfall reports indicated that the *Dalniy Vostok* had, instead, changed course again—this time heading southward, as though to double back around the nearly completely exhausted *James Bay*. Captain Korotva and navigator Herron furiously plotted curves on charts, pushing against the mathematical reality that set the limits of our movements. Was it still possible to intercept the fleet? Several hours and fuel checks later, the answer came back. No, not without leaving ourselves stranded at sea without fuel, without food, without water.

On August 27, the *Dalniy Vostok* completed her loop, well to the south of us, and began to trek eastward again, carrying her flotilla of death machines with her. The *James Bay* was now too far along her great circle route to Winter Harbour to give chase. Winter Harbour was four days from us, and the margin of fuel had shrunk to the point where there was no other point of land we could reach.

Powerless for the moment to do anything except follow her trajectory to Vancouver Island, the *James Bay* continued to cleave the water smoothly before a following sea while the air changed rapidly from the last hint of the tropics to early Pacific Northwest autumn. Now we found patches of fog. Bathing suits, shorts and T-shirts disappeared and out came sweaters and jackets. Sandals gave way to running shoes and boots.

Before we reached shore, Dr. Spong completed his analysis of our efforts. He reported that "In four direct actions—confrontation situations—the *Greenpeace VII* mission saved in the neighborhood of thirty to forty sperm whales. These were whales that were being hunted at the time of confrontation and which escaped, at least for the moment, as a result. Additionally, the close presence of the Greenpeace vessel to the Russian whaling fleet during ten days of contact and chase forced the *Dalniy Vostok* factory ship and nine killer vessels to steam far faster and farther than normal. Instead of slow, systematic sweeps, the Russian fleet was forced into erratic, rapid movements as it attempted to evade the Greenpeace vessel. This must have made the whole Russian operation much less efficient than usual. The killer boats scattered rather than working in teams for the immediate pickup of single, instead of many, dead whales after each kill which is usually the case. Assuming a conservative kill estimate of twenty per day and twenty percent Greenpeace interference impact, this factor adds an additional fifty sperms, at least, which were also directly saved as a result of Greenpeace efforts. In all, the *Greenpeace VII* mission directly saved a total of perhaps ninety or more sperm whales. Valued at roughly $20,000 each, this theoretically represents a loss to the Soviet whaling industry of $1.8 million. This is roughly two percent of the industry's gross annual income."

Dr. Spong continued, "Besides these live whales which were directly saved by Greenpeace presence in the areas where they were being hunted, it is clear that neither the Soviet nor Japanese fleet ventured any closer to the North American west coast than 800 miles, whereas for over a decade, until last year, the *Dalniy Vostok* had slaughtered whales within seventy-five miles of the shoreline. It is too coincidental to think that they stopped hunting these grounds—which are among the richest remaining whale-populated areas—for any reason other than fear of exposure. Until Greenpeace's arrival in their midst, their activities had remained a public secret, unknown even to active U.S. antiwhaling organizations. Greenpeace can at least take credit for having brought the glare of public attention to bear on the fact that whales were being slaughtered virtually off the beaches of North America, and both the Russians and Japanese chose to avoid any further unwanted attention. Until this year, an average of 1,300 sperm whales were annually taken by whalers from waters closer than 700 miles to the U.S. and Canadian coasts. Unless the sperm whale population in those areas has been decimated, we may reasonably estimate that 1,300 sperms did not die by explosive harpoon within that 800-mile zone, a zone which may now be said to be under the 'protection' of an alerted North American media and public. This large number of individual sperm whales may be considered to have been indirectly saved by the Greenpeace mission. Directly and indirectly, the *Greenpeace VII* mission saved a total of probably 1,400 whales."

Above, cameraman Ron Precious after a confrontation with the Russians. Below, musician Mel Gregory

Susi Leger kneads bread in the
galley.

Walrus Oakenbough and Ssor Thornwood
at the bow of the *James Bay*. The trip
is ending . . .

Sunrise landfall at the west coast of
Vancouver Island

Postscript
Rex Weyler

It was the magnetism of whale consciousness that carried us like a wave so far beyond ourselves, and whale magic alone that kept us afloat through this stormy story that perhaps will never really end.

During the winter of 1976 George Korotva and Paul Spong went back to Hawaii, where they joined forces with local environmentalists to raise funds toward the purchase of a boat for the next year's assault on the whaling fleets. Walrus Oakenbough, Kazumi Tanaka and Taeko Miwa went to Japan and there they spoke with whalers, whaling company officials, politicians and citizens, urging them all to join the growing global movement to save the whales.

By the time the 1977 summer whaling season began, three expeditions were underway to shut them down. From Honolulu sailed the *Ohana Kai*, a 170-foot former U.S. Navy subchaser. The *James Bay* sailed out of Vancouver, and in Australia, Greenpeace Zodiacs took on the land-based whalers which operated out of Albany at the southwestern tip of Australia.

In Australia, Jean-Paul Fortom, Jonny Lewis, and a band of whale people followed the Cheynes Beach whaling vessels out from their land station, traveling by compass beyond the sight of land. Twice the Australian whalers fired past the protesters, once so close that the propeller of Jean-Paul's little boat snagged on the cable between the harpoon and the wounded whale. The local motorcycle gang, "God's Garbage," and the mayor of Albany found a common ground in defending the people's right to make a living by killing whales.

The *Ohana Kai* ("Family of the Sea") dogged the Russian factory ship *Dalniy Vostok* for a week, traveling over 1,200 miles north of Hawaii. In that time no whales were killed, because no whales were seen. Our worst fear, that the whales were already too close to extermination to recover, was beginning to look painfully justified. At one point, the crew of the *Ohana Kai* desperately set out to board the factory ship. They drove their Zodiacs right up the stern ramp of the *Vostok*, and clambered up onto the flensing deck. Spong, Kazumi, Nancy Jacks, and Dexter Cate greeted the shocked Russian crew with whale buttons and Russian-language literature explaining that hundreds of thousands of people all over the globe were asking them to please stop killing the whales.

On board the *James Bay* we stalked the second Russian fleet for two weeks, catching up with them 800 miles off the coast of Baja California. Here the Russians finally came upon some whales. A small pod of eight sperms was spotted early one morning and pursued by a harpoon boat. During the next four hours we frustrated the hunt by staying between the whales and the ships. One by one, every ship in the fleet joined the hunt until a total of ten harpoon boats pursued the one pod of whales. Finally the lead boat fired past us, missing us and the whales as well. As the panicked whales were forced to the surface, the boats closed in. Harpoon explosions sounded all around us as we realized our helplessness. They slaughtered every whale in the pod: bulls, females, and calves.

A month later we too boarded a Russian ship, a killer boat that was tied up alongside the *Vladivostok*. I went on board with Pat Moore, Bob Taunt, and our Russian translator, Rusty Frank. Rusty spoke fluently with some friendly Russian crew members, telling them who we were, why we were there, and asking them how they could possibly justify scouring the oceans to kill the last of the great whales. The whalers agreed that they had found very few whales that summer, and they accepted our gifts of whale pins and buttons with warmth. After our encounter, we all felt that we had finally punched through the wall that separated us from these other human beings, somehow cast as whalers in this crazy movie in the middle of the Pacific Ocean.

We sense that we are near the end of the era in which human beings unwittingly slaughter the whales to the brink of extinction. In Japan hundreds of workers are laid off each year as the industry winds down. The Russians have indicated officially that they are soon to stop whaling. At this writing the International Whaling Commission has been forced to lower the quotas in light of the unexpectedly low catch figures. But what a grand day it would be in the evolution of human consciousness if we could collectively decide to stop killing the whales now, not for economic or political reasons, but because we were finally able to see through the barrier of specism that has separated us from all the other sentient beings with whom we share this planet.

Many people have already made that breakthrough. They are the whale people, and the motifs of their stories indicate some mysteriously shared shift of consciousness, brought on by their encounters with the whales. Suddenly we see ourselves face to face with an alien intelligence right here on planet earth. And perhaps we have heard the signals that mark the end of the childhood of the human race. Perhaps we have begun to break the bonds of our humanness, and to accept ourselves, not separate from, but as a part of wild nature.

Greenpeace has been a small part of this global movement not only to understand the whales, but to save them. And the people on these pages are only a small part of Greenpeace. To thank, acknowledge, or even know all the people who have had a hand in materializing this collective vision would be an impossible task. We have each done what little we could, and through that collective effort there are whales alive in the sea today that would otherwise be gone forever.

San Francisco
November 9, 1977